D0913061

MICHALINA
Daughter of Israel

Rachel Sarna Araten

MICHALINA
Daughter of Israel

AM YISRAEL CHAI PRESS, Jerusalem, Israel

First published 1986 • ISBN 0-87306-412-7

Copyright © 1986 by Rachel Sarna Araten

Am Yisrael Chai Press, Jerusalem, Israel

Distributed by:
PHILIPP FELDHEIM Inc.
200 Airport Executive Park, Spring Valley NY 10977

FELDHEIM PUBLISHERS Ltd.
POB 6525 Jerusalem, Israel

Dedicated to
all the daughters of Israel
who have the wisdom and the foresight,
the courage and the faith to make their home
in the Land of Israel

Acknowledgments

My debts of gratitude are out of all proportion to this short book.

I am under great obligation to Michalina's youngest brother, who placed at my disposal the entire relevant correspondence between himself, his brothers and sister.

To my nephew, Dr. Jonathan D. Sarna of Cincinnati, I owe thanks for much of the historical material on the work of the missionary nuns.

My lovely sister, Aviva Miriam Segal of Ofra, went through the first typescript with a stern — and constructive — red pen. From my one-time colleagues, Avraham Harari and Schmuel Reem of Jerusalem, I received invaluable practical help and much encouragement.

And above all, there is the debt to my husband, not measurable by any standard. For months and months he had to listen to the tap-tap of my typewriter at all hours. With unflagging patience and unfailing good humor he has read and reread and read yet again every page of the manuscript as often as I corrected, restyled and rewrote. "Thank you" isn't much of a word for all this.

R.S.A.

Contents

Introduction

Not long before her death, Hannah, Michalina's sister-in-law, paid a visit to her brother and was there introduced to an elderly acquaintance of his. This man, on hearing Hannah's married name, said in surprise that he knew the family, he had lived next door to them in Cracow and had played with the boys in *cheder*. So many years ago that was!

Then he suddenly remembered something else and asked, "By the way, did you ever hear anything about that girl who was kidnapped, their sister? What happened to her?"

Well, that is what this book is about. The story must be told, for "he who is able to write a book and does not write it, is as one who has lost a child," said the Bratzlaver. It is, indeed, the story of a child who was lost — but regained. It is an account that should be restored to the national memory — for its beginning, which should never have been allowed to happen, and especially for its end. That has its own meaning.

Just after *Chanuka* in the winter of 1959, Yehuda, a resident of Haifa, traveled abroad on a study tour. A fairly frequent traveler, he could have had no inkling that this trip would result in much more than increased knowledge. Yehuda adhered to his program until the summer of 1960, when an unexpected change sent him to a conference in Amsterdam. Here he met a non-Jewish professor from Italy, whose attention had been engaged by Yehuda's family name. He invited Yehuda to take a ride with

---

The name Michalina is an affectionate form of Michal, who was the daughter of Saul, first king of Israel.

him one night through the canals of Amsterdam, and there he asked a strange question: "Do you have any relatives in Warsaw?"

Yehuda looked at him, puzzled by the query, and the other proceeded, "Your name is an unusual one. My father's brother married a girl with that family name way back in the early years of this century. My uncle died long since, but his widow lives in Warsaw with her son."

Thus, simply yet dramatically, did Yehuda learn the whereabouts of a sister who had been completely lost to her family since the *Chanuka* of 1899. When he wrote about it to other members of the family in Israel and New York, a spate of zealous curiosity helped to unearth a long-forgotten history, details of which were then found in issues of old, extinct newspapers of the year 1900, the Zionist weekly *Die Welt* and the Cracow-published Hebrew paper *Hamagid L'Yisrael*.

Michalina's is the story of a frail human being, frail not in herself but in her helplessness in the face of a power that, unhampered by any other might or human consideration, was able to take the child out of her natural surroundings and transform her into a creature of a foreign world. Certainly, this girl, far from being frail, had been made strong by growing up in the warmth of a harmonious family in a loving, strictly religious Jewish home. She was possessed of a fund of obstinacy that looks clearly out of her eyes and speaks from her lips in the earliest available photograph of her, a passport photo taken when she must have been in her early teens. "They" had bandied her about from pillar to post like a packet of mail and in the Poland of those days a passport was needed for that. Her face at this time is smoothly, childishly oval. The abundant hair is brushed back severely except for a wave that dips over one side of her brow in a willful streak of vanity. The large eyes stare at the photographer steadily, even a bit defiantly, but the well-formed nostrils seem to quiver; one can almost see that those full lips will soon tremble into a paroxysm of tears as her endurance gives way.

She must have needed all her strength of will to enable her to adjust to the strange world into which she had been thrust. She learned to live in this world until she knew no other, until a deliberate process of brainwashing, followed by a complete amnesia, wiped out any consciousness that she had once been a natural part of a different world.

How could it have happened? One can repeat this question again and again. Had Michalina's been a single, unique case, the question could have been answered with a murmured remark about the lunatic fringe of society, or something to that effect. But Michalina, a child of thirteen and a half, was abducted from her home simply because she was Jewish. Her kidnappers neither expected nor did they gain any monetary advantage from the theft of this child.

Max Wurmbrand and Cecil Roth, in their book *The Jewish People*, that tells how our nation survived during the four thousand years of its existence, relate that in the nineteenth century

> ...there were from time to time deplorable cases of kidnapping of Jewish children for baptism. Though formally unofficial, they were subsequently endorsed by the Church. The most notorious instance was the Mortara case in 1858.... It was late in the day for such a flagrant abuse....

Michalina was kidnapped from her home in 1899 — still

later in the day!

The circumstances of the kidnapping deserve a more thorough examination than the mere telling of a story, even at the risk of some apparent digressions.

The nineteenth century was an era of change in all spheres of life. It has been called the "Great Age of Christian Expansion" as well as of awakening humanitarianism. But as the adage has it, "paper is patient"; it bears words that sound fine so long as one refrains from analyzing just how their content affects human lives.

It may even be pertinent to ask how far the Christian expansion and humanitarianism went in setting the stage for steady improvement in the ways of men. A claim to greatness should be justified. But the answer is discouraging: today we have to admit that our world is one of unbridled violence. Lust and greed are its mainspring, and little pretense is made at idealism. Day after day, the cinema, television, books, magazines and newspapers tell of all forms of human debasement. There is scarcely anything today too low or too degenerate to be accepted.

In full knowledge of human history, men coldly occupy themselves with devising methods of destroying their fellows in masses. Rich natural resources are unashamedly exploited to make possible the holding of entire and powerful nations at the end of the blackmailer's noose. The greatest of horrors, the most evil of them all, was allowed by a Christian world* to spread its insidious poison with impunity, so that little headway has been

---

*A report in the London *Jewish Chronicle* of February 15, 1985, tells us that "The Rev. Robert Ellis — an Anglican clergyman — in a paper he wrote, 'The Holocaust and the Christian Conscience,' said that the churches must not only accept responsibility for creating anti-Semitism, but had to acknowledge that they failed by allowing the Holocaust to occur."

made against the spirit of Nazism even today.

One can in these days observe something like a conscious repudiation of human dignity that surely goes hand in hand with self-hatred. And, possibly, that is progress of a sort. For in the yesterday which this story recounts, the era that saw the dawn of humanitarianism in a great era of Christian expansion, men trampled on their fellows in the name of what should have proved an ennobling force, the force of religious fervor.

No claim can be made that the decoying or abduction of young girls from the homes of their parents is an act that ennobles, whatever the purpose. In Cracow alone, in Austrian Poland, at least thirty young Jewesses were to be found incarcerated in cloisters towards the end of the nineteenth century. There were at least thirty Jewish mothers and thirty Jewish fathers with unbearable heartache — and there were possibly more, in other places, of whom we have no exact record. It is hardly likely that any of these captives are alive today, more than eighty years later.

Let this story of Michalina, a daughter of Israel, speak for them all.

Part I
The Beginning

MICHALINA was the first-born, beloved daughter of a well-to-do Chassidic family living in the ancient city of Cracow, then a grand duchy, part of the Austrian crownland of Galicia. Cracow has been described as the most interesting city of Poland, with its many old and historic buildings and its many national relics. At the end of the nineteenth century this ancient capital was still "the intellectual center of the Polish nation," a description worth remembering during the reading of this narrative. Over ninety thousand people inhabited the town at the time, including a large number of Germans in addition to the Poles, and something more than twenty thousand Jews. The town had thirty-nine churches for the spiritual edification of its inhabitants, as well as twenty-five convents and monasteries.

More interesting to us is the Jewish quarter of Cracow, the suburb of Kazimierz, where Jews have lived since the fifteenth century. Until the Hitler period Kazimierz had been an important Jewish center with well-known *yeshi-*

*voth** and a number of highly interesting synagogues; their description would fill a book itself, both for their history and their architecture.

On Szeroka Street stands the oldest synagogue of the community, known as the "Stara" (meaning "old"); it was built in the first part of the sixteenth century and has always served as the focal point of the Jewish life of Kazimierz. Its most interesting feature is its sunken floor which, to the Rabbis who approved the building plan, seemed to invest with realistic significance the psalmist's cry: "Out of the depths have I called Thee."

About a hundred meters from this old synagogue, at the other end of the street, adjoining one of the suburb's three cemeteries, is the most famous house of prayer of all, the Rema, known as the "new *shul*"; it was built in 1557 on the site of an older one that had been destroyed by fire. The Rema is named for one of Cracow's most famous scholars, Reb Moshe Isserles. While the earlier building had been made of timber, this new one used brick and stone; its walls are immensely thick and it has beautiful accouterments. In its storage coffer the synagogue wardens preserved, together with various records and the holy ornaments, the *Seder Haftoroth* (known as the Haftor Manuscript) which had been donated in 1666 on the occasion of what the Jews vainly hoped would be "the imminent redemption of Israel."**

Reb Moshe Isserles was a man of wide learning and literary achievement; his greatest contribution to Jewish scholarship is his *Mappah*, the notes he appended to the *Shulhan Aruch* — Joseph Caro's *Code of Jewish Law*. By means of these glosses Ashkenazi usage was added to

yeshivoth — academies of talmudic study.
**The appearance of the false messiah, Shabbtai Zvi.

Sephardic practice, thus making the *Code* the authority for Ashkenazim and Sephardim.

Until the German invasion, it was the custom on Lag be-Omer, the Scholars' Feast, for thousands of Jews to visit the Isserles tomb in the cemetery near the Rema synagogue, where the graves of the scholars of Cracow are to be found. Although the building suffered damage during the war, it has since been restored and is still in use but, of course, Cracow's Jewish community has greatly dwindled.

Nor was constructive work in the Jewish quarter of the town confined to that of centuries back. As late as 1928 a modern Jewish academy was established and in 1934 the Beth Yaacov Seminary was set up for the training of Jewish girls as teachers. This was, of course, well after the period of our account here, but it is important to underline the vitality of Jewish culture and tradition in the place where Michalina spent her girlhood. This is the framework from which she was torn.

Michalina's father, Reb Yisrael, was a scholar, a gentle, sweet-natured man, well versed in Jewish lore and learning. He was an adherent and disciple of the illustrious sage and great teacher, Rabbi Aryeh Leib Alter of Gur, known as the Sfath Emeth (the language of truth). It was Reb Yisrael's custom to rise well before dawn every morning in order to study Talmud for a few quiet hours before the other members of the household rose. His wife had borne him three daughters and four sons of whom she was wont to say, "Each of them is my only child."

It was a close-knit family basking in the mutual sunshine of affection shed over the home by such parents. The children were intelligent and the atmosphere intellectual, and no effort was spared to inculcate in them all, boys and girls alike, a love of learning, of the things of the spirit and of the beauty of Torah and Jewish humanism.

Reb Yisrael's greatest enjoyment was to sit with his children in the quiet evening hours and expound a chapter of the Mishna, the Jewish legislative writings, making his point with an allegoric tale to ensure the interest of the young minds. He laid particular stress on the teaching of *Pirkei Avot, Ethics of the Fathers*, in order to guide his children's daily conduct towards those around them. "Behave always like a *mensch*, a human and humane being," he would exhort them, "and so you will be true to your Jewish heritage."

The great dream of the family was to leave the Exile one day and go up to the Land of Israel "from which all holiness emanates." Strictly observant though the parents were, there was nothing of stern dogma or of bigotry in their make-up, and the Jewish life of the home was joyous in the Chassidic fashion, easy and unforced, as natural as the air they breathed.

★ ★ ★

And here we come to the real beginning of our story, for us the real beginning, since we can only guess at the organizing and plotting that preceded it.

It was the end of December 1899, the time of *Chanuka*, the Jewish Feast of Lights, which commemorates the rededication of our Temple in Jerusalem after its defilement by the enemy. *Chanuka* has always been the time for families to draw together in the winter twilight. In all the cities and hamlets of the Jewish East European world, families would gather in the evenings around the heated *kacheloifen*, the large tiled stove, to enjoy hot potato pancakes and drink fragrant lemon tea from the samovar.

In Michalina's home, as in other Jewish homes, an air of geniality, comfort, and affection pervaded the pleasantly furnished living room of their large flat during this winter festival. Outside, in the cold streets, only a few days had passed since the Christmas festivities had reminded every Jew that no matter how many generations he and his family had dwelt in the place, it was at best a temporary home, a mere booth, not ever a place to be taken for granted. Less than forty years later this was proved to the Jews of Cracow, too late for practical usefulness. Fifty thousand Jews were living there in 1939; seven hundred remained by 1970.

Back in the nineteenth century, the wassails and carousing of the celebrant Christian citizens of the Slav world only too often erupted into bouts of Jew-hatred that ended in anti-Semitic violence. During that entire century there had been ritual murder charges, pogroms in Polish towns, and sudden expulsions from Russian towns and hamlets. At the time, there was hunger in the larger part of Galicia, with Jews in their hundreds dying of starvation almost daily. And if the Jews of Cracow were spared such calamities for the time being, they but turned more fervently to the God of Israel. The drunks who shouted "Christ-killers" in so many places could touch neither the pride of good Jews in the memory of their glorious Temple and the heroism of the Maccabees, nor their faith that God would, in His own time, restore His people to their sovereignty in the Land of their Fathers. Recalling the verse in Isaiah, "Comfort ye, My people, saith your God," Jews found comfort in the idea that God called them "*My* people."

So Michalina's father, like most Jewish fathers, took out the brightly polished, beautifully wrought *menora* —

the eight-branched candelabrum — and joyfully lit the *Chanuka* candles while the voices of the whole family filled the room with the sound of the melodious "*Ma'oz Tsur*," the song that so vividly recalls outstanding episodes in the national history of the Jews.

Shabbath Chanuka, the Sabbath that falls during the festival, was treated as a special day; both parents would go to the synagogue together with the older children, all festively dressed. But this year, 1899, their live-in housemaid, who had only recently been taken into the household, had asked for the day off, and Michalina, thirteen-and-a-half years old, was left behind, perhaps to keep an eye on the younger children. Yehuda, the youngest brother, was but a toddler. It may be that the pretty, intelligent girl was not so pleased at having been left at home.

Possessed of an enthusiastic nature, she liked the joyful Chassidic praying and the tuneful liturgy. She may have been glad when the housemaid invited her to take a short walk in the clear winter weather. This servant was a Catholic woman who wanted to show her young companion something very special. She had no admiration for the Jewish synagogues, believing that her own church and the services she participated in must certainly be finer than those of her employers. So Michalina went for a walk with her—and never returned to her parents' home.

Far too young to realize that the servant was an agent, one of many planted in Jewish homes by church authorities, the child accompanied the woman confidently enough. She was curious to see this "most beautiful" place that was promised, though the woman gave the child no hint of what it was.

Churches were, indeed, architecturally finer than synagogues, mainly because most Christian governments insisted on their being so. Synagogue builders were obligated to put up structures that were simple and unostentatious, and that were lower in height than any churches in the vicinity.

But in any case Michalina was not taken for a walk in order to look at fine architecture. She was taken straight into the convent of the Felician nuns, where the doors were quickly closed behind her, hermetically so. The servant, however, was sitting demurely in her room when the parents returned from synagogue. She denied all knowledge of Michalina's whereabouts, saying that the girl had just gone out for a short walk. But as the afternoon wore on and she observed that worry and even panic were overtaking the household, she managed to slip away unnoticed.

Later, when the suspicion of a Catholic police officer fell upon her, she was found and arrested for abduction of a minor. She then broke down under interrogation and admitted that she had taken the child for a walk and had shown her the church. According to this servant, Michalina had merely peeped in, had then been pulled inside by force, and had not been allowed to leave. There is no record of the woman ever having been tried and punished.

Sixty-three years later, on a small farm in Israel that had been made to flourish out of arid, long-desolate sand dunes, Michalina made her only reference to that far-off day: "*Dieses abscheuliches Ding, dieses Dienstmaedchen*" ("That despicable thing, that servant-girl"), she said.

That remark barely hints at the suffering caused to Michalina and her family by those who conceived the plan which they sent their agent to carry out. For even in the English language, rich as it is, it is hard to find words expressing something of the pain of parents whose children have been torn from them.

Today, living as a free people in our own ancient homeland, we, the generation that felt the jackboots of the Nazis and witnessed the gas chambers, do not hesitate to take stern measures to defend our children (especially when *katyushas* are fired at us from across the borders). And the world has found a cliché: the Jews of Israel have a "Massada complex." Israeli Jews, the world feels, tend to "overreact," not merely when they are threatened, but worse, when they are attacked—and the world is shocked.

But the Jews of Israel are the links in the chain that binds the present generation to everything that happened to our people. Even if we possessed a short national memory, we would be hard put to it to merely "react," or perhaps — to suit the needs of nations living peacefully within their own borders — to "under-react."

Blood libels, a feature of past centuries, sent Christendom into wild passions of hate and revenge, revenge for deeds that had never been committed. But the stealing of Jewish children — and Michalina was one of many — left that same world callously cold. We witnessed similar reactions during the Hitler period and even long after the establishment of the State of Israel.

The purity and sanctity of family life was the cornerstone of Jewish survival during the long centuries of exile from the ancestral homeland. Our sages teach that a youngster is ripe for the marriage canopy after the age of eighteen; accordingly, Jewish sons and daughters were often married young, and in the special circumstances of Jewry in the countries of its dispersion there was great wisdom in carrying out this precept.

Of course, technically — if the word may be used in this connection — the practice did much to ensure the continuity of the nation. But there was more to it than that. For one thing, in marriage young people found a chance for self-expression in a world whose claustrophobic living conditions and restrictive laws stifled the development of natural potential. Suffice it to mention the *numerus clausus* of the universities as an example.

Then, too, the affection of home life provided a solid shelter in a hostile environment, while the Jewish way of life gave a spiritual and ethical framework to sustain morale in times of trouble. By taking in the young couple for a specific period as the custom went,* Jewish parents gave their newlywed youngsters the chance to grow together in all respects before they had to take on the burden of facing an unfriendly world for their own livelihood. The custom could not have been uniformly successful, but it did form the basis of that inner strength which is the gift of harmonious family life. The masses of Jews throughout the Diaspora, and in the Slavic lands in particular, whether poor or wealthy, had no assets more precious than their children. They were not merely a personal source of deep satisfaction, they were always the future of the nation. For the Jews this was life itself.

Such had been the background of Michalina's parents, now in their mid-thirties, young people still, when disaster struck. The sister and two brothers who were born after it always described how happy their childhood and adolescence had been. No hint of bitterness on their parents' part had ever been allowed to mar their lives.

---

*The custom of giving the young couple board and lodging was known as giving *kest*.

The End of One Way

COMING BACK from the synagogue that *Shabbath Chanuka*, Reb Yisrael and his wife waited in vain for their eldest daughter to come home for the festive meal. *Havdala*, the ceremony marking the end of the Sabbath and the onset of the working week, is made early during the short days of December, and the parents, not knowing what it was that the vague fear in their hearts portended, went out that same Saturday evening to ask the Cracow police for help in looking for their daughter.

The next day, December 31, they were told that the housemaid employed in the household had induced the child to enter the convent of the Felician nuns.

Accompanied by a police constable, Reb Yisrael went to the convent at once and demanded to speak with his daughter. The convent mother, Sister Marie Rosalia, acceded to his wish and went to bring her. The footsteps of the child were heard as she was brought to the other side of the iron grille that partitioned the room, and then the waiting men heard her burst into uncontrollable weeping. Her father never forgot how she begged, "Father, take me home, I want to go home." He could repeat the words years later in the same intonation, as well as the rejoinder of Sister Marie Rosalia, "Come back in another five days. It is important that your daughter gets used to us before she can be allowed visitors."

In *The Book of General Laws Pertaining to Citizens of Cracow*, paragraph 145 provided for police assistance to be given to any citizen whose children had got lost or were unaccountably missing from their homes. Under this paragraph, parents had the absolute right to see and speak to children who for any reason had left or been taken from their homes. The police were enjoined to take all needful steps to return such children to their families. On the basis of this law, Reb Yisrael applied to Police Director Korytkiewicz. His response came in these words, "What? You expect *me* to take a girl out of a convent?"

The father persisted, knowing himself to be within his rights legally as well as morally. His daughter's place was at home with her mother and siblings. His wife was making herself ill with grief. She would wrap a dark shawl around herself and go out in the chill air of the early mornings to stand near the convent building in the hope of getting one of the passing nuns to show mercy and let her see her own child, her first-born.

The poor woman could not understand what had come upon their happy family. Her thoughts turned to the picture of them all. Her children were clever, God be praised, and made good progress in their studies. On Friday nights, with all of them in their Shabbath clothes seated around the festive table with its wine goblets, the braided golden loaves and the special meal, there would be laughter and singing and friendly teasing, and then the children would listen attentively as their learned father instructed them on the weekly Torah portion. The mother's heart was full of deep pride as she recalled that weekly scene.

Other pictures arose. On *Purim*, the Feast of Lots, which fell when the first signs of spring appeared, they would act out the story of Esther and Mordechai, having rehearsed it for weeks in advance. Oh, the pride and pleasure of the grandparents who made up most of the audience! *Pesach*, in contrast, was an affair of grandeur and solemnity, ushered in by weeks of complicated preparation; only by the stern discipline of hard work would the Jews of the Exile grasp the meaning and value of freedom, that will-o'-the-wisp.

But when summer came round, they would all troop off to spend the hot months with their grandparents out in the country, roaming the green fields and forests and taking in the beauties of nature. Not many Jewish children were so privileged, and all of hers grew to adulthood imbued with a love of flowers, plants, and trees. She herself, this bewigged matron, loved greenery and smiled as she remembered how her second son, Avraham, liked to pick a flower to pieces, petal by petal, in order to find out what made it grow, what was inside it that caused it to be so pretty. (Michalina herself watched him do this sixty-three years later in Jerusalem. The flower remained a mystery to him all his life and he always saw in it the wonder of God.)

Then why should these unmarried women, these nuns, want her daughter? The mother's thoughts never wandered far from this question. When the evening grew too cold for her to wait passively, she would timidly stop a passing nun and beg her, "I shall always pray for your well-being, only please, please, let me have a glimpse of my child."

Such entreaties fell on deaf ears.

At last, after days of stubborn insistence at the police offices, Reb Yisrael was granted permission to return to the convent together with Police Commissioner Toma-schik, but Sister Marie Rosalia was ready this time, too. Michalina, she claimed, was ill and therefore could not see anyone. (A father may not visit his sick daughter?) The police commissioner replied that the girl's mother was now gravely ill and asked only to see her child once more before the illness took its fatal course. Again the worthy nun had a reply, "She will see her child in heaven."

Reb Yisrael then immediately set about getting medical advice for his sick daughter, and managed to bring two doctors to the convent. These were the university professor Dr. Zulawski and the doctor attached to the law courts, Dr. Filimowski. They were allowed to examine the child and declared her to be perfectly fit.

Days full of activity pass too quickly. The father tried every possible avenue to get his daughter returned and this ceaseless exertion brought with it its own momentum, but the mother was stunned. It just did not seem possible that this thing was happening. What was the child doing now, she wondered. Was she cold? She had taken no clothes with her that day. Were the nuns caring for her? To the mother, these women didn't give the impression of being overly kind or compassionate. Was the child being properly nourished? Was she eating their forbidden food? She couldn't bear to think about it. The girl must be terribly homesick, she was only thirteen, after all. Was she not longing for her sisters? For her baby brother? And again, that nagging question that had no answer: What did the nuns want with such a child? Why wouldn't they let her out?

For there had been other such cases, many, in fact, though they could not recall one of a child so young. This stealing away of Jewish young women was the latest of the tribulations of the Jews of Poland. It was gradually becoming known that in a great many of the cloisters of Poland and Galicia young Jewish women were being held and baptized so that their children, after forced marriage to gentile men, would be born "into grace." Alternatively, if it could be done, the girls were trained to become nuns.

It was also known to the Jews of the region that officers of the army with glittering uniforms and cavalier ways were able to lure Jewish girls from homes where they observed Jewish law but were not taught the Jewish holy lore and so could not be expected to appreciate their spiritual heritage. But this was not the case with Michalina. She and her sisters had received the same Jewish education as their brothers.

Michalina's mother knew no rest, neither of mind nor of body, and meanwhile the days were passing with no apparent progress. Her daughter was kept as if in prison. It was exactly this passing of the days which was deliberate for, according to Christian custom, a child attains its religious majority at the age of fourteen when it no longer requires the permission of its parents to choose its way of life. Michalina would be fourteen at the end of May.

Her father's efforts, however, were not entirely in vain. On January 22, 1900, Police Commissioner Tomaschik received orders from his superiors to demand that Sister

Marie Rosalia yield up the child. He was told to make it plain to her that the law could enforce the execution of this order. This time, too, the worthy nun, good soul, had her answer ready. It was received in silence by the police commissioner who wrote it down verbatim in the protocol he prepared for his superior officers:

> We shall make certain that when the case comes before the court, it shall be held up and drawn out until the child's fourteenth birthday, when no legal obstacle will stand in the way of her baptism. Meanwhile, she will be removed from here to another place.

On January 29 Reb Yisrael was asked to come to the police authorities; they handed him a notice they had received from Sister Marie Rosalia stating that on January 27 Michalina had run away from the convent of the Felician nuns in Cracow. This was a blatant untruth.

In the meantime, the case had received a great deal of publicity in the press. The Hebrew newspaper of that time, *Hamagid*, reported that all of Austria's liberal press had come out unanimously on the side of the family, while the anti-Semitic papers were making mock of Reb Yisrael and expressing glee at the trouble that had befallen the Jew. (So peculiar these Jews, my dear! Simply put a man's daughter into a convent and he runs about like mad trying to get her out. Can you imagine it?)

Many friends of the family as well as men picked by the family's lawyer took turns watching the convent gates from a distance. Witnesses reported that two nuns, one of whom was named Isidora, had taken the girl away and brought her to the affiliated convent of Lagiewniki near the district of Podgorze. The gendarmerie of the region confirmed the presence of the girl but did not intervene, since they lacked direct orders to do so.

In 1962 when Michalina, then an old lady, returned to her family in Israel, she had no recollection of any of this. She bore no memories of having been taken from place to place, nor did she remember what these places looked like or who took care of her there.

"I lie awake nights," she would say wearily, "and try so hard to bring back some kind of picture of it all, but it is one great blank." One is reminded of those large staring eyes in the passport photo. Had they drugged her before removing her?

Methods

THE FELICIAN nuns of Cracow appear to have taken upon themselves the task of bringing as many Jewish girls as possible into the embrace of Christianity. They had perfected a number of methods to this end, some of which were described in those old issues of the newspaper *Hamagid*. On July 26, 1900, this paper published an article on the topic, part of which is quoted here (freely translated from an old-style Hebrew):

> Indeed, it is now known: The Felician convent in Cracow is the focal point for the hunting of the daughters of Israel in the towns and small villages throughout the districts of Poland. Hunters and hired agents go stalking Jewish girls to take them captive, and the nuns place their reliance on the inertia and indifference of the courts, which enable them to increase their activities and hold in captivity as many girls as they possibly can. A casual glance at such cases might give the (mistaken) impression that

the nuns merely give shelter to a few empty-headed girls in love with non-Jews, who come of their own accord. The more recent cases, however, clearly show that the nuns had themselves initiated the pursuit of these girls and hold them by force....

This very week we have learned of the following instances: on Yom Kippur (the Day of Atonement) last year, three peasants came to the house of the widow Chana Weiser near Tarnow. The widow was in the synagogue at Tszetotsin while her daughter was alone in the house. The peasants abducted the young woman and brought her to the nuns in Cracow. The mother came over there in terrible fear but all her efforts to get her daughter released were futile. At last, the widow became gravely ill and had to be confined to bed.

In Dovsziza two dressmakers cajoled the daughter of one Elija Mendel into going to Cracow. Her father came after her but the nuns would not let him see his daughter. When the unhappy man pleaded with them tearfully, they sent him to the governor, Prince Posina, who in turn sent the man to the ministry whence he was referred to the police — and it was all in vain.

Another Jewish girl from Szwirezcov succeeded in escaping from her captors after suffering their torments for three months. She told of two more girls from Russian Poland who were being held then in the Felician convent and who sat and cried all day long.

Yet another case is told by a Jew from East Galicia about his aunt and sister, two obedient, trusting young women. One was employed in the house of a lawyer in Lwow, the other was in her parents' home in Husziatyn. Somehow, they became acquainted with two gentile young men and were soon persuaded that a deep love had flowered between each pair of the quartet. These two men promised to marry the girls who, with this in view, left their homes and went to Cracow to meet their lovers. After spending some hours wandering about, the men claimed that because of the lateness of the hour they were unable to find a priest who would perform the marriage ceremony. As the girls had in the meantime used up such little money as they had on food, and had nowhere to go for the night, the men came out with "a good idea": if the girls went into the convent just for that night they would be given a meal and a bed. The marriage could be performed the next morning. For lack of a better solution the girls went — and saw neither their lovers nor their own families again!

The nuns would never release any girl until they had made absolutely sure she would remain a Christian to the end of her days. But should it happen that they had their doubts about a girl, they would arrange for her to go into domestic service in the home of a priest who would then keep an eye on her with a view to completing the work of the nuns. This is what happened to the man's aunt. His sister had not the strength to withstand the nuns and allowed herself to be baptized. They then married her to a Christian laborer in Podgorze, adjoining Cracow. This man was an illiterate drunkard who hardly earned a penny, and her life with him was one of great poverty and terrible hardship.

A similar fate has befallen most of the girls captured by the nuns. Parents are never allowed to enter the convent to see their daughters but brothers are sometimes allowed in. The Galician Jew who told about his aunt and sister had been permitted to visit inside the convent: he had been received by a nun who, with tears running down her face, pleaded with him to emulate his sister and so effect the salvation of his soul as well.

According to the writer of this article, the Galician Jew was only permitted to see his sister in the presence of a nun; he could not talk privately with her. He saw a number of girls, who looked pale and blue, exercising in the grounds of the convent. One hour of exercise per day was all that the nuns allowed. Through a gap in the hedge, he managed to get some information from one of the girls.

He learned that their daily routine began with an hour of prayer in the early morning, after which they were

The convent of the Felicians in Cracow

given one glass of milk. Then they were set to work at various tasks until noon. Their midday meal consisted of some vegetables and bread. Prayers until two in the afternoon were obligatory. After an hour of exercise, the girls spent the rest of the time laundering clothes. They had a glass of milk and some dry bread for their final meal of the day. From this dry routine there was no respite whatsoever until, after baptism, the girls consented to marry one of the men the nuns had chosen for them, or were sent into the house of a priest.

The nuns also had more drastic methods. During the time that Michalina was known to have been held in the Cracow convent, witnesses noticed a young girl — perhaps it was even Michalina — who had apparently been allowed to take a walk by herself outside the building in the late twilight. As she began to walk up the road, a woman suddenly rushed towards her from a side alley and began to scold and slap the child in great anger and passion. The girl cried aloud in astonishment, "Mother, Mother!"

But it was not the girl's mother — she had been dressed to make this impression in the fading light. For almost at once, two nuns came speedily out of the convent and "rescued" the girl; as they took her in by the main gates, the "mother" was seen to slink in by a side door.

Later investigation of the very few who had managed to escape revealed that similar beatings and "rescues" were carried out in the dead of night during the few hours of sleep permitted the girls. After their "rescue" they would be indoctrinated with the idea that the Virgin Mary was a kinder mother who would never beat them so long as they believed in her. "Thou shalt not love thy mother" was a tried measure for weaning young girls away from their natural affections, as will be shown further on.

Over sixty years later Michalina told her family, "I know nothing about my mother. The nuns in Ypres told me I was an orphan and that the Virgin Mary was my only mother." And when asked how she had come to be in Ypres in Belgium, she had no recollection of any journey.

In Cracow, however, during that winter of 1900, her mother was in a state of anguish that even bereaved mothers do not feel. The death of one's child is final. Somehow one has to come to terms with it. But to know one's child is alive and to be forcibly kept apart for no other reason than one's Jewishness is a different kind of suffering.

The Search

UPON LEARNING that the child had been removed to the Lagiewniki cloister, Reb Yisrael lost no time in petitioning the district governor of Podgorze to order the release of his daughter. This official first had to make a trip to Lwow (Lemberg) in order to consult the *Stadtholder*, Count Pininski, and by the time he returned, Michalina had been spirited away from there.

The pious, God-fearing Jew now realized that he had no alternative but to journey from one convent to another. No sooner had he learned of his daughter's new whereabouts and arrived there than she was taken elsewhere. He found himself at the cloister in Binczice; from there he went to Morawice, and from there to Wolajustowa. Then he traveled to Kenty and on to Wielowies — and in each place the doors of the convents remained closed to him while the civic authorities refused him all assistance. An exception was the mayor of Kenty who made an attempt to get the legal rights of the father recognized. For this the mayor was accused of disturbing the peace and was sentenced to ten days imprisonment. On appeal to the court at Wadowice this sentence was lifted.

The next step was described in a letter that Reb Yisrael wrote to the Polish newspaper, *Slowo Polskie*:

> I heard that my daughter is in the convent near Tarnow, and I sent someone to ascertain the truth of this. When this man told me that he had twice seen my daughter, I went there with an acquaintance. We had not yet arrived when we were both arrested by the police of Tarnow on the pretext that we were unable to identify ourselves. After some fourteen hours I was set free and at once I went to the district governor to lodge a complaint and also to tender a request that I should be allowed to enter the convent. This governor sent me to the district judge who answered that he could do nothing without a direct order from the attorney general, so I had to go home from Tarnow as empty-handed as I had come. My friend is still held there under arrest.

The letter went on to tell how one of the ministers applied to had informed the unhappy father that orders had been sent to all the church authorities in Austria, forbidding them to baptize Michalina before her fourteenth birthday. This gave Reb Yisrael a slight ray of hope that he could still effect her release before that date.

But as this case and similar ones attracted more attention, the authorities of Galicia became annoyed with the father's persistence. Count Tarnowksy and a Dr. Ziel lodged a strongly-worded complaint with the president of the Ministry of Justice: the impertinence of these Jews, they indignantly declared, was insufferable. By what right did Jews dare investigate convents? They should be punished for this, and Reb Yisrael in particular, for this outcry was at his instigation. He was punished, heartlessly so:

Reb Yisrael asked for and obtained an audience with the minister of justice, Baron von Spens-Booden, who told him that he could go home and be confident that his child would be restored to him. The baron had sent orders to the Cracow municipal authorities that the law pertaining to the abduction of children was to be carried out, and Michalina was to be returned to her parents. Cruel as it may seem in view of the baron's promise, these orders were rejected.

The chairman of the city council, President Moralewski, authorized an official letter to be sent to the family's advocate, Professor Dr. Joseph Rosenblatt:

Reference number <u>VIII 395/900</u>
155

Without taking any decision on whether the applicant in this matter is to be considered as having a private interest in it, judgment in the affair of Michalina is withheld because there are important reasons which hinder it.

The letter was dated March 29, 1900 and bears the signature of one Wawrausch signing in the name of the Court of Penal Law. What were those "important reasons"? No one could find out, for no one would reveal them.

The family appeared to have come to the end of the road. The minister for Galicia, Dr. Pientak, whose intervention had been asked for, stated bluntly, "All worldly power stops before the walls of the cloisters." This would give the impression that behind the walls of the cloisters there was a heavenly power. Yet, the power behind the walls was wielded by mortals.

One possible strategy still remained untried and Reb Yisrael did not hesitate to implement it. He asked for an audience with His Imperial Majesty, the Kaiser Franz Joseph in Vienna. It was with the latter's express permission that the Motherhouse of the Felician Sisters had been established in Cracow in 1865 after its suppression by the Russian government in the wake of the Polish armed insurrection of 1863. The Felician nuns did valuable work among the poor and the homeless, especially in education. Michalina, of course, had never been a homeless girl. Reb Yisrael was hoping that the Kaiser Franz Joseph would understand this and wield his influence. The audience was granted. Cautiously optimistic, Michalina's father made the long trip by train to Vienna. He placed his faith in the God of his fathers, praying throughout the journey that this "king of flesh and blood" would be more humane than the Church authorities. There was hardly anything more that he could do.

On April 26, 1900, a month and a day before his daughter's fourteenth birthday, Reb Yisrael laid aside his customary Chassidic garments, donned the tailored black suit and top hat ordained by court protocol, and made his plea before the Kaiser. In a voice almost uncontrollable for the tears that choked his throat, he implored the Emperor of Austria-Hungary to intervene so that his child would be released.

The court photograph of this Chassid dressed for the occasion shows a dignified, upright figure with brooding eyes and a worried, stern face, an expression that no one had ever seen on this gentle Jew. In a portrait of him as an old man nearing his ninetieth year, the expression is completely different: the eyes are clear, inquiring, alert,

Reb Yisrael
at the court
of Emperor
Franz Joseph

and intelligent. His mouth is set in a smile of good humor. One can clearly see that this Jew had never allowed himself to become bitter or to lose his interest in life. His faith in the God of Israel never deserted him, and his suffering bound him more closely to his Jewish way of life.

The facts of the case had been made known to the Kaiser beforehand and he must have known exactly how far his power went and that it stopped before the gates of the convent. But he was alive to the personality of this man before him, and if he knew himself powerless, he would be kind just the same.

"I will send new orders to the authorities in Galicia so that they shall carry out their legal obligations and do their duty," he promised.

As Reb Yisrael learned later, the orders were indeed sent out within two hours of his reception. But even the Emperor Franz Joseph was powerless before the hostile walls surrounding Michalina.

On May 8, the district judge in Cracow, Edmund Hartmann, told Reb Yisrael, "Go to the attorney general, let him give the order — and we shall see that it is thrown out as it has been hitherto." Close to despair, the father went to the Ministry of Justice on May 17 and again on May 19 when he was promised by Baron Spens and by Dr. von Koerber that everything would be done to ensure Michalina's release before her fourteenth birthday. These were mere empty words. For the time being, the church seemed to have won out.

The New Way

THEY MUST HAVE baptized her, with or without her consent, as soon as she reached her fourteenth birthday. She could never remember it, nor had she any recollection of this period. Her earliest memories were of a convent in Ypres, in Belgium, where she was sent, probably, immediately after the baptism, when it had become apparent that her family would not relax its efforts to regain rightful control of her. The nuns changed both her given name and her surname so that she never again answered to the name Michalina.

She became someone else. In Ypres the nuns made sure that she thought she was an orphan and must always be true to her fatherland, Poland. The rules of this convent were very harsh, and the friendless girl hated it. Letters came to her regularly from the archbishop of Cracow, exhorting her to do her duty meekly and submissively as befits a true Christian daughter, but they could not alter her rebellious attitude to this place. At last, possibly sensing that if they wished to keep their hold over her, it was vital to gain her cooperation, the nuns transferred her to a convent in Bruges. This must have been a convent school for better-class girls; she remembered a dancing teacher who came in from Brussels every week to give the girls lessons in dancing and deportment.

It is rather puzzling that Michalina was treated so differently from all the other Jewish girls who had been forced into baptism and coerced into marriage with boorish native peasants in Galicia and Poland. Was it because she was exceptionally pretty and intelligent? Or because of the persistence of her parents in trying to get her back? Or was there some hidden purpose? What were the "important reasons" mentioned in that letter signed by Wawrausch? They were obviously known to the authorities.

Who can or would answer these questions?

Whatever the reasons — and at this point in time they no longer matter — the helpless girl was more fortunate than most. She finally settled in to life in the convent at Bruges, which suited her temperament. During the two years she was there, she took full advantage of the good education it offered her, and she was able to matriculate at the early age of sixteen.

During these two years they turned her into an accomplished young lady, with dainty habits, polished manners, and a certain dignified poise. She finished her schooling speaking a cultured Polish, fluent French and German, and adequate English. She could dance gracefully and do fine embroidery and sewing. She was also very patriotic. Years later, she never tired of telling her family how she had been praised for her recitations of Polish poetry in class and for her essays on Polish history and literature.

Predictably, she was then sent back to Poland where employment was arranged for her with a wealthy, aristocratic Polish family living in Gola near Posen. The sixteen-year-old convent graduate became French tutor and governess to the fifteen-year-old daughter of the family. Their extensive estate was supervised by an agricultural engineer. This thirty-three-year-old bachelor lived in the neighborhood, was quite a rich man himself, and had an eye for a pretty face and figure. For the present he remained unknown to the governess.

One wonders what kind of personality had developed from the three distinctly different worlds to which she had been exposed — the laughter and warmth of her Jewish, Chassidic home, then the long series of convents, and now the life of the aristocracy amongst whom she earned her bread. Each was a small, closed, self-contained world, and the gaps between them were apparently unbridgeable.

Her employers in Gola must have been satisfied with their "find," for after a year, when they decided to make a grand tour of America and England, they took the governess with them. To Michalina this journey must have been like going out of a terribly long, dark tunnel into light. She would say later that this trip abroad gave her a taste for travel that she never relinquished, but perhaps there was some deeper motivation for her invariable eagerness to go traveling as often as occasion offered. Just now, of course, it offered her a chance to see a world quite different from anything she had known. It also offered her the chance to wrench herself free once and for all from the surveillance of the nuns and the discipline of the convent. This opportunity came in the form of a romance that, outside novels, was unusual in those days, when "like" generally mixed with "like."

Whom should they meet while traveling in vast America but their own supervisor from Gola, who soon joined their party. In such a closed circle he could pay attention to the handsome young governess in a way that would not have been *comme il faut* at home. He went on to England with them and there he proposed marriage to her. He was thirty-four and she was barely seventeen, but the church gave its blessing and they were married there and then in London.

Though one might prefer to suppress it, a question arises here. Was the meeting of engineer and governess pure coincidence? Was this hasty marriage in London planned by members of the church in order to prevent intervention by Michalina's family in Cracow? Ironically, although her children would be born "in grace," thus achieving the aim of the church, through this marriage Michalina took the one step to freedom that in the long run would loosen her ties to those holding her in their grip. But that was yet a long way ahead.

Six decades later, after Michalina had returned to her family and was living on Mount Carmel in Haifa, her son Karol wrote a letter to her brothers — addressing them not as uncles but as "Highly esteemed brothers of my mother" — in which he described his father's death bed in 1926 when Karol himself was a young medical student. "My father," he wrote, "tried hard to tell me something that was very important to him, but he was so ill and in such pain that I would not let him speak, and at last he died without mentioning the matter."

No one can know what it was that lay so heavily on the engineer's mind. But Karol's letter was written a lifetime later. For the time being, seventeen-year-old Michalina

Michalina at the time of her marriage (left) and as the "grande dame" in Poland (right)

had achieved the most that she could possibly have expected. The former governess now found herself back in Gola, this time as the supervisor's wife. This "poor orphan girl" whom the nuns had befriended now had a staff of servants to attend to her every wish in a fine house with beautiful gardens. She had elegant clothes and jewelry, and she lived a life of comparative luxury which she enjoyed all the more after the spartan years in the convents.

On Sundays and Saints' Days she went to church, properly clad in her Sunday clothes. She followed all the rites of the Christian festivals faithfully and carefully. Of

Christian philosophy, of the meaning of Catholic doctrine and ideology, she knew nothing. She had probably been taught it, but perhaps subconsciously she had rejected it.

Her son was born ten months after her wedding and a daughter a year or two later. Motherhood was blissful for her and she was now a happy woman, having lost nothing but her real family, her memories and her natural childhood.

In their place Michalina had a variety of activities: she sat on all the social committees of the neighborhood, tremendously pleased that what she was doing was for the good of Poland, her fatherland. There were pleasant summers at resorts such as Zakopane; there were entertainments and excursions and society. There was little wrong with life any more — apart from the strange moods which came over her from time to time. During these moods, she became so restless that nothing would please her but she must be off on a journey somewhere or other.

Her photograph at this time shows a face full of intelligence and character. From beneath eyebrows that are delicately and beautifully arched the large eyes gaze pensively at a world to be kept at a slight distance from her. Her mouth has become firmer. Despite the hint of passion in the full, curving lips, there is the slightest expression of disdain, if not of triumph, at its corners. Her hair is fashionably dressed, the high-necked, well-fitting gown is elaborately embroidered. There are pearls around her neck and, in lieu of a belt, a gold chain with a locket around her waist. This is a girl full of charm — but not one to be taken liberties with. Her stance seems to say, Don't dare touch or approach me, unless I permit.

Fleeting Moment
of Truth

IT WAS PERHAPS inevitable that one day Michalina had to face up to the fact that she was not an orphan.

Perhaps in compensation for the loss of their eldest, a daughter was born to Michalina's parents and two sons were born later. Michalina's mother found some consolation in her renewed motherhood. Nevertheless, she and her husband were never able to put their first-born child out of their minds, nor were they willing to give up the search entirely. When Reb Yisrael heard that Michalina had been taken out of the country and sent to Belgium, however, he settled down to his usual routine and spoke to no one of any activity he initiated through his friends abroad.

Reb Yisrael knew that in the various convents of the Cracow district Michalina had been an unmanageable child and that the nuns had a hard time taming her. Certainly, she was not the material of which nuns are made; she had been too used to being governed mildly with love to take kindly to the austere discipline imposed on her by strangers.

With the help of friends and relatives in various Jewish communities he followed his daughter's progress as best as he could. He even once received a letter bearing the postmark of Ghent in Belgium, supposedly written by her though the handwriting could not be verified. This letter advised her father that she was happy in her new faith and suggested that he take the same path! Although he replied to this letter and also wrote several times afterwards, his letters were never answered. When one of his sons left Galicia to settle in Belgium a few years later, Reb Yisrael entrusted him with finding his sister. But his attempt was futile since she was already back in Poland.

This, too, became known to Reb Yisrael. He succeeded in getting her address and he secretly contacted her, asking her to meet him at a hotel in Breslau. The family only learned of this meeting from Michalina herself a lifetime later, but by then she was too old to recall the exact date. It must have been sometime between 1904 and 1905.

But she remembered how the summons had shaken her up. A father? For years it had been drummed into her that she had come into the care of the nuns because she'd been orphaned. Past memories, they had taught her, were sinful because they were deceptive. This was a lesson she had been forced to learn thoroughly. And now, as if she suffered from a kind of chronic amnesia, pictures would come and go in her mind and she could not interpret them.

Despite her fears of sinning, she took her infant son and went off to Breslau to meet this father. At the time she could not have said whether she went out of curiosity or some subconscious yearning. Nor could she articulate her own reaction upon seeing the man who came towards her, unmistakably Jewish in his Chassidic garb, somewhat hesitant and uncertain. He held his arms out to her as he approached. One look and she knew it was her father. She had seen such a face in her dreams, had heard that gentle, tender voice and felt the love now shining in his eyes.

But why then had she always been so alone? This was something she could not understand. He looked so kind though his eyes were very tired and his face had a worn, ascetic appearance. What was he saying? Something about her coming home with him. She could live with other relatives if she felt her own home was too strictly Orthodox. All this was unintelligible to her. Orthodox? What did he mean? She was a very strict Catholic. And where had he been all those years ago when she had cried herself to sleep in the harsh convent of Ypres?

After at least five years away from all Jewish learning and influence, Michalina could not know that a Jew, once baptized, is mourned for as if dead because such a Jew is in reality lost to his people. A child taken early out of school will soon have forgotten most of what was taught. Knowledge if not pursued is quickly lost, and so it was with Michalina.

Nor was there any way for her to know how much heartbreaking effort her father had put into finding her. That had been carefully kept from her. By some well-tried method, the memory of that day on the other side of the grille had been blotted out. While she was still fully aware of things during the beginning of her incarceration in Cracow, she must have been puzzled that none of her large family came to take her home. Her gaolers had easy answers to this, easy and convincing answers since for so many years she had seen and heard nothing of her parents.

Her father would not call her by her new name. Clinging to the name he had given her was the only way he could grasp that this elegant, poised young woman was the naive, merry little daughter he and his wife had taken such pride in.

Reb Yisrael, seeing his daughter for the first time since she had been taken from her home, did not realize how her memory had been tampered with. He tried to talk to her of the past, of her home and her brothers and sisters. His first words were "Your mother..." but she stopped him short. Then, in a flash of insight, she realized that she could not tell this man that her only mother was the Virgin Mary. She could not bear the hurt in his face, she could not look into his eyes which were brimming with tears, she could not endure the pain and compassion she saw there. She pointed to her little one and said in very gentle tones, "It is too late. I might have gone with you but I am married. I must be with my son and he belongs to his father. We have to return to Posen now."

He would not tell her how his wife longed for the child she had lost. Reb Yisrael knew full well that had Michalina gone with him, "they" would have found a sure way to take her own child from her. He could not subject his own daughter to the same bitter suffering he and his wife had endured; so all he could say to her was, "My child, remember your real name and who you are: Michalina, daughter of Israel." He put his hands on her shoulders for a minute, then turned and left.

The search was now finally over. He had seen his daughter again, in health and contentment. He could not take her by force and had to understand, however reluctantly, however regretfully, the reason for her decision.

His responsibility henceforth would lie, doubly so, to his own people. His refuge would be, as always, in his beloved holy books. Not long after that meeting he moved his family away from the bitter memories of Cracow to Vienna where they lived for some years. After World War I, they moved farther north to the Low Countries. Two daughters had married and remained with their husbands in Cracow. As for the others, their great dream was realized when, some ten years after the war, Reb Yisrael settled in the Land of Israel. He was soon joined by some of his sons and his youngest daughter. After living in Tel Aviv for a time, where his wife died, he moved to Jerusalem to be with his son Avraham who was building his home there.

As a child of thirteen, he had taken a piece of parchment and in his fine script had written out the selected Torah verses for the *mezuza*. Reb Yisrael was privileged now to nail this *mezuza* to his doorpost in Jerusalem. He settled down to compile anthologies of Chassidic teachings and Jewish ethics, work that filled his life to the end.

Meanwhile, the years passed and no further contact was made so that Michalina, busy with her children and her social activities, could only think — whenever she allowed herself to think about it — that if she had a real family, they never troubled themselves about her. Once she commented, "Since that day in Breslau when I saw my father, I have known nothing of a family."

But shortly before his death in 1957 (only three years before she was discovered by her brother Yehuda), Reb Yisrael told his son in Jerusalem, "I know she is alive, my heart tells me so." His eyes were wet, and in a broken voice he added: "Had she died I would not today be feeling the pain of her so deeply. My tears would have dried up."

This gentle, pious Chassid had been well tried by the God in Whom he had never lost faith. During that half century, two wars had turned the world into one great, bleeding, poisoned abyss. One of his sons had died of wounds inflicted by Arabs rioting in Jaffa, while his two married daughters had had the breath choked out of them in the gas chambers of Auschwitz.

But no one in Gola knew that the lady of the engineer's mansion was a Jewess, and although she took part in the struggle against Hitler, it was as a Pole that she did so, and she came through it all. Not that fate spared her completely. Her husband died in 1926 and thirteen years later her only daughter died of tuberculosis. Michalina, too, knew the pain of losing a daughter.

Part II
Start of Something New

I F YEHUDA'S TRIP to Amsterdam that summer was unexpected, the question of the Italian professor he met there was even more unexpected: "Do you have any family in Warsaw?"

Yehuda's mind gave a lurch. He found it difficult to concentrate on what the man was telling him about his father leaving Poland to settle in Italy and about the uncle who had married a girl with the same family name as Yehuda. Yes, there had once been another sister, but he could not remember her. She had been much older and she had not been talked of at home. Could it be? A very old lady, widowed now? Was a crazy fate playing some trick on him?

Then he recollected that his older brother, Avraham, in Jerusalem had told him of their father's certainty that the eldest daughter was still alive. He also recalled a very long, serious conversation that their father had once had, years and years ago, with their other brother who was leaving home to settle in Antwerp, and whose letters at the time caused cast-down looks and disappointment.

So Yehuda sat down now and listened avidly to all that the Italian could tell him. He decided he would get in touch with the professor's widowed aunt, despite the risk of mistake or rebuff.

The first contact was made by Yehuda giving his Italian colleague a short note and a photograph of himself to send to Warsaw. He wrote to Michalina in German, since this language was the closest to the Yiddish they had all used at home. In the note Yehuda explained how he had come to hear of her, and he added that he was ready, indeed eager, to visit her before returning to Israel.

Michalina received her nephew's message with the enclosures from Yehuda on August 8, 1960 and at once sat down to write to him:

> I saw my father once about fifty years ago or more but that was the only sign of life I ever had of a family. My brother's letter has shattered me — but it is best that he does not come to visit me here in Poland. You don't know the Poles [she tells her nephew enigmatically], you have always lived far from here. It would be an enormous happiness to meet my brother but not in Poland. If you invite me I would come at once. Without an invitation one cannot travel out of Poland.

She was seventy-four years old at the time. Her first reaction was one of unquestioning acceptance — she had a brother, and she was ready to meet him.

She continued the letter by giving some details of her life in Warsaw where she had been living for the last ten years with her married son. She explained that a great deal of her property had been requisitioned during and after World War II, which was the reason she moved from Posen to Warsaw. She wrote that she maintained her financial independence (at her age!) by teaching French.

Suddenly, in the middle of writing these everyday details, it struck her that something out of the ordinary had happened, and she wrote:

> My brother's letter and still more the photo he enclosed have "brought me out of my skin." I am completely stunned.

Then she became more practical:

> So if you invite me I shall come at once. I have been standing before the mirror and comparing my face with my brother's photo but can find no similarity. [She was wrong in this; as soon as one saw her with her brothers the family resemblance was evident.] A man looks different from an old woman. First I must see my brother, I *will* see him, and then I shall know what I feel towards him.

A whole psychological process was now underway. The next day, after a sleepless night, she wrote again. She had been so excited the day before that she feared she had not addressed the envelope correctly and the letter would go astray. By that time the news had penetrated more deeply. She wrote:

> Your letter was shattering for such an old woman as I am with my very weak heart. Even now I am unable to pull myself together and think logically. I have not been able to get a moment's sleep, my head is throbbing. I recall the poem *"Die Lorelei"* — do you know it? — and the lines run in my head: "I know not whence my sadness...."

And then she paraphrased a line, underlining the words thickly with her pen:

> *"Ein Lied aus alten, alten Zeiten kommt immer wieder in mein Sinn."*

(A song of old, old times returns again and again to my mind). Had she misquoted because of an uncertain memory — or really purposely paraphrased? Nothing later ever gave a clue to this. Her letter continued:

> I am normally a fairly strong person but now I am completely beside myself. I knew nothing of my family. The last time I saw my father was more than fifty years ago and I was already married and a mother. I think this is the first time in my whole life that I am so entirely shaken up. My hand trembles so much that I cannot write steadily. For such an old woman as I am, that news was something that tore me apart. I am really very old... you will not recognize your quiet sensible aunt in these lines. I no longer know myself since I got your letter. If you can hand over this letter to my brother, disjointed as it is, then please do so. My hand trembles so strongly and the words seem to be swimming.

One must bear in mind that in this first flush of excitement she was entirely alone. "Knowing the Poles," as she says, she had to keep the matter to herself. Though she never said it explicitly, she was unwilling at that point to admit even to her own small circle of friends her close relationship to a Jew. Not being able to confide in a single living soul at such a time must have been a great hardship.

Two weeks later she wrote a third letter. Her tone had changed, the euphoria had vanished. Possibly she had had a confrontation with her son, for though none of her letters mentioned this, she did tell her brothers about it after meeting them, saying then that he had been put in very bad humor when she admitted her Jewish origins.

She felt bad, she wrote in this third letter, because her blood pressure had gone up. She recalled a traffic accident in which she fractured her skull, and she mentioned that it had begun to hurt her again. She couldn't imagine herself able to leave Poland that year for all sorts of reasons. "To put it briefly," she declared, "no one can call me robust any more."

There was an element of fear, of withdrawal. Postponement seemed to be the best policy for the moment, and she enumerated some of the problems: it takes so long to get a passport in Communist Poland, letters take ages to arrive, there are certain financial conditions set by the government which have to be complied with, and so on.

She consoled herself and her brother: should she live so long, which she doubted, she will try to meet him next year if he takes another trip to Europe. And then, like a stroke of lightning, the phrase "meet my brother" flashed upon her understanding, and she wrote:

> I cannot understand how my brother could remember me. I believe, to tell by the date, that he was hardly three when I left my parents' home. I feel very pessimistic today.

The very next day, however, she wrote a fourth letter, addressed to her nephew as all her letters had been so far. She repeated all the problems connected with obtaining a passport "so that, unfortunately, nothing will come out of this whole matter." This time however, she enclosed three photographs for "my beloved brother"! She had forgotten that she had to meet him before she could know her feelings for him. These photos of her had been taken many years ago:

> Today I am an old woman and much too vain to have my photo taken. Old ladies, however, are in reality much prettier than they look in pictures.

Her eagerness to make a good impression on her newly

found brother was touching. Again, forgetting that she had addressed the letter to her nephew, she asked:

> Dear brother, does my photo remind you of your little sister?

She was, of course, at least ten years older than Yehuda. But she must have been looking at that first passport photo while she was writing.

One week later, a telegram arrived from her nephew inviting her to visit him in Italy (she needed an invitation in order to travel outside Poland). The idea of traveling again put all fears out of her mind. She replied by return, in a letter full of plans, stressing the very great pleasure it would give her if her brother could meet her in Vienna and they could go on to Trieste together. She added:

> You know, dear nephew, that I have always been a very self-controlled person but since this news came I am beside myself. I cannot pull myself together just now but you know that in general I am no hysterical woman. Don't show this to my brother, he will think I am always like this.

Less than twenty-four hours had passed before she was at her writing-desk again. She claimed that her letter of yesterday was senseless ("*unsinnig*") and that she had been too eager about the arrangements for the journey. In the meantime she learned that travel was impossible. She had spent the whole of the previous day trudging from office to office in Warsaw and wherever she went the result was the same: there was no way of leaving Poland just yet.

There is something in the picture of this determined woman going from one office to another so that she could see her own brother that is reminiscent of her father going from one convent to another and from one authority to another so that he could see his own daughter. With a sigh of resignation she concluded,

The joy must be postponed for some months.

Then there is a pathetic attempt at humor:

In order not to disappoint my brother too greatly I shall have a photograph taken of me after all so that he will see he has not lost anything much, I am only an old woman... I am joking because my heart hurts at not being able to meet and greet you...."

Here, for the first time, she refers to her brother in the second person. But she refers to herself in the third person:

Despite her age, your sister is still capable of many illusions... one may never give up hope.

Is the use of "her" instead of "my" evidence of the trauma she has experienced as if she has lost awareness of who she is? Or is it a sign that she still cannot speak face to face with her own flesh and blood?

One thing is clear: the idea of having a brother was becoming a reality for her. Hardly had she added her signature to that letter and sealed the envelope than she began another letter — this time addressed to Yehuda:

Lieber, lieber Bruder, ("Dear, dear brother") although one can hardly remember him, it is a wonderful feeling to have a brother in the wide world. I am too shattered to write. You cannot know how much pleasure your letters give me... I have put your photo in my little room and every day I tell you "good morning" and "good night."

After many weeks she had finally begun to live with the knowledge that she had a very close relative. She began to take pleasure in communicating with him, even imagining bringing herself to meet him in person one day!

And Back to Something Old

T HIS IS ALSO the point where her innermost feelings are suddenly in a state of upheaval. She begins to feel that her pleasure in having a brother may be of a mixed quality. Despite the strange self that had been imposed on her, she never lost the basic integrity of her early upbringing. Was it not her own father who had taught her in her childhood, "Keep thyself far from false speech," and "Where there is no truth, there is no peace"? If she had long forgotten the actual teaching, the lesson had not been lost, and building a good relationship with this newly found brother under false pretenses became distasteful to her.

She wrote him a letter of over 300 words, this old lady with her trembling hands. The thoughts she expressed had been running through her mind for several days. Writing them down, she said, "has cost me nerves." But she was possessed of strong will power and was determined to do what she thought was right. Her letter, in part, reads as follows:

I write so often in order to give pleasure to myself
and to you. But I have unhappily omitted to tell you
my "credo." For sixty years I have been a Catholic
and I shall die in this faith. Also I am a Pole and have
done very much for my fatherland. These two points
are inseparable from me. Perhaps you thought that I
was quite indifferent to such things as my nephew is;
this is not so. And since I am quite well-known, I
must tell you that it would give me no pleasure at all
to have you visit me here in Poland. My son would
certainly not like it. It would make him unhappy on
account of his wife if you were to come to Warsaw.
It hurts me to write this but I feel it my duty to do
so. And duties have often to be carried out with a
bleeding heart as in my case. Dear brother, don't be
angry. I must be open and truthful with you.

Michalina then hastened to reassure her brother of her
love for him and of her happiness at his having found her.

"I am so very alone," she wrote, and with what men
might call feminine inconsistency, she proceeded to tell
him how beloved she was by her Polish family and grandchildren, how very popular she was with her pupils, and
how many good friends she had.

The letter ended with a plea. Using his name for the
first time (and one wonders if it meant anything to her),
she begged him:

Dear Yehuda, don't misjudge me and don't think
badly of me; my dear boy — I may call you so, you
are so much younger than I am — don't hang your
head but forgive your sister and think of more pleasant things. Life is sometimes so short that it is
hardly worthwhile. When I have my photo taken I
shall think of you so that my love will find expres-

sion in my face. If you are not angry with me, then write.

A few days after she posted this letter, her brother received a number of letters she had written earlier, that had accumulated while he was traveling. (He had put off his return to Israel for a short time, hoping that perhaps he could go to Poland.) He answered these before getting this declaration of her "credo" and, as usual, she replied to him immediately:

> Since I got your first letter, I have hardly slept. Neither Phanador nor any other sleeping pill helps me. I am only half awake by day and converse with you quite a lot. Today, for instance, I looked at your photo in my little room and asked you: "Why do you write that my early photographs and my handwriting are similar to those of *your* mother? You should have written *our* mother."

This comment is significant although she did not then realize the implication of what she had written. When she came to live with her Jewish family in Israel, she had to go through a painful process of reconciliation with the memory of the mother whom she could not remember at all. She had to undo the work of the nuns in regard to this, for had they not taught her, and taught her thoroughly: "Thou shalt not love thy mother"? But to return to her letter:

> You can imagine how tired I am after such nights. Have you ever read *The Call of the Blood* by Corvin? I read the book a great many years ago and now I find myself thinking of it over and over again. If my previous letter has reached you by now you will see how strong-willed I am. But believe me, I love you sincerely, the same blood runs in our veins as it does

not in those of ... (here she lists a number of names in her immediate circle in Warsaw).... I shall be so happy to see you and your wife but my place is here in Poland. I could never have believed that I could be so torn, that there would be such discord in me.

Apparently, her decision to remain Catholic and to stay in Poland was not quite such a self-evident matter as she would have liked her brother to think. That last sentence revealed more than she realized or intended. In her next letter, she again reminded Yehuda of how very old she was and added that it had never occurred to her that a loving brother would brighten the last moments of her life. It would be wonderful for her to see him in the coming year and go back to Poland knowing she had him in this world. It was, she mused, a strange feeling to have a brother, to be aware of loving him and yet not to know him. She had had her photograph taken by then and had sent it on to him. She was most curious to know whether this snapshot, taken in her old age, would remind him of "our" mother as the early ones had. However, as she wished to meet him in person, she thought it was necessary that her brother be able to recognize her. Fearing that he might not be able to do so from the photo alone, she added a description of herself:

> I am of average height with brown eyes and silver-grey hair, an oval face and I weigh sixty kilograms in my clothes. Nose and mouth normal — neither too small nor too large. The worst are my legs for I have broken both of them twice over and had them in plaster-of-paris for weeks.
>
> So now, when you close your eyes, as children say, you can see me as I am though you have never seen me. Please tell me, if you can write once more before

As an old lady in Poland in 1960 (left); four years later, after the meeting in Italy (right)

you leave Europe, if I at all resemble my mother. Her face is entirely unknown to me. But I recall my father very well for I saw him in Breslau fifty-two or -three years ago.

This fact is repeated again and again in her letters.

Meanwhile fifty-five days had now passed since Yehuda's first letter filled her whole being with silent disruption. For the first time her mind was so attuned to her peculiar fate that she asked him to tell her about "those who belong to us." She was curious to know all about "the living as well as the dead." And, above all, "I must meet you before I die."

Nevertheless she had a moment's hesitation. Sensing

that her newly-found family might demand of her more than she was prepared to do, she added:

> I am unusually sentimental today. But you must bear in mind that letter which demonstrated my strong will power. Perhaps my heart beats more quickly than is normal today and this puts me in such a soft-hearted mood. My next letter will read differently.

As with all her letters, this one was signed not with the name her father had given her — Michalina — but with the name bestowed upon her in the convent.

The face in the latest photo still bore traces of her youthful handsomeness but her eyes had a different expression — they no longer held the world at arm's length. The mouth was the mouth of one who had much to battle with in her own self. As it happened, she still had a long way to go.

For the moment, part of that way still lay through the mail. The letters went back and forth, and Michalina's scrupulous tactfulness made itself noticeable. She never wrote that "our letters crossed" — which happened often enough, since she seldom waited for a reply but wrote whenever the urge took hold of her. Instead, she would write that "our letters probably met each other somewhere on the way." Furthermore, when she finally met her brothers and later came to live with them, she never crossed herself, although this must have been second nature to her.

But now her brother Yehuda was to return to Israel, and she began to express some uneasiness about receiving letters which contained an Israeli postmark. Letters, cards, small gift packets suddenly arriving with a regularity unknown before that summer and autumn of 1960 could only attract attention which she preferred to avoid, and she toyed with the notion of having her letters addressed to a niece of her late husband who "would know for whom they were and would not open them." She made every effort to take a room for herself and move out of her son's flat, but this was no easy thing in the Communist world.

In any case, a woman of Michalina's age could hardly make a journey to Italy without the knowledge of her son and his family. So, as Yehuda's return to Israel drew nearer, she threw all caution to the winds so far as her son, family, and friends were concerned and began to make serious, meticulous plans for a trip to Italy in the coming spring. She wrote of these plans in the greatest detail again and again, as if the very repetition of them maintained her belief in their being carried out.

Meanwhile, she received from her brother an account of their family. Earlier, she had asked for such an account "somewhere on the way," as she had put it. Not wishing to upset her at this distance, Yehuda had given her only a brief outline of what had happened to her. She reacted with one short remark, "I can't imagine how it was possible." But she was immensely happy to receive her brother's description of their father. "You have given me great pleasure with this," she wrote.

She began to read the trilogy about Josephus (Feuchtwanger's *Jewish War*). This was the first time she displayed interest in anything Jewish.

"You know that I am a Catholic," she said in one of the last letters she wrote before her brother left Europe, "but you don't know how I thank my God that we have found one another."

By this time, Michalina had been put in contact with

her other brothers, and was corresponding with them, too. Shaye, born after she had left Cracow, had traveled a great deal and described something of his journeys in his letters. This elicited her most impulsive response. She answered that she had taken an atlas and had carefully traced the route her brother had taken, and then she had read about the places he had visited so that she now felt as if she herself had accompanied him. She wrote that she had also been an impassioned traveler for as long as she could remember; she had been to many lands, had wandered through many great cities and had visited many museums and exhibitions. What she did not write about, but what came out later when she got used to talking to the various members of the family, were those moments of restlessness and the puzzling gleams of memory that would on rare occasions break through the fog of amnesia that cast a veil over her early years. Her marriage had freed her from the spartan convent discipline, but not from those unaccountable moods. At such times she would feel an urge to go on a journey though she couldn't have explained why. Accompanied by her husband or brother-in-law — the Italian professor's father — she had even visited Cracow. As she had wandered through the streets there, faces had appeared to her as if through a mist. As she had looked at the people in the streets she would try and recognize someone but she had not known to whom those wraithlike faces belonged or even who these people were for whom she was searching.

Such trips always brought disappointment, causing the amnesia to settle more completely. These sudden gleams of light always ended with her feeling annoyed with herself for an apparent lack of purpose. In time, the intervals between one mood and the next became longer and the flashes of memory vanished more swiftly. Then she was left with an overpowering desire to go abroad which she could not explain. As often as it was possible she would accompany her husband on his business trips or would visit his family in Italy, until Hitler's war put a stop to her traveling.

Now, after all those years, Michalina was marking off on her calendar the days before she would stand face to face with men born of the same parents as she was, and she would know "what she was feeling."

At Last

YEHUDA completed his arrangements for the first meeting with his sister during the spring of 1961. He felt it best to make this first meeting as brief as possible. He wanted her to become acquainted with him and his wife Hannah and then have time to herself before the next meeting. He himself was none too calm about this encounter, and a short first talk would not be too overwhelming in either direction. He therefore decided that they would meet for one day. Then he and Hannah would travel on for a week's visit to Yugoslavia where he had a professional conference to attend.

Yehuda was hoping that his two younger brothers would manage to join him in Italy after his return from Yugoslavia. Their presence would show Michalina something of the warmth of her own original family life and would help to ease the atmosphere between the newly introduced family members.

As for Michalina, her eagerness to get to know her

brother Yehuda only partially overcame her apprehension about the venture. It is not so common for a woman of seventy-five to leave her home and take a journey across Europe in order to meet someone who had declared himself to be her brother.

Never having traveled by plane, she wanted to fly to Vienna, but her grandchildren, some of whom were doctors, would not permit this. So she took the train and arrived in Italy a few days before her brother. Meanwhile she stayed with her niece, the sister of the professor who had brought about the reunion. In the first week of May that year, as the day of the meeting drew near, she found herself in a greater state of trepidation than she had thought possible. She telephoned her nephew, asking him to come to Trieste to be at her side. He made the ten-hour journey from central Italy in order to support her during the first meeting.

Yehuda, for his part, could not sleep for nights beforehand. He thought about his parents and how it would have been had they still been alive. After all, it was barely four years since the demise of their father, who had remembered Michalina in his very last hours. Yehuda's nerves finally got the better of him and he was terribly sick the whole night through, after getting in to his Trieste hotel late one Sunday night.

No more than sixteen years had passed since the second World War had ended and Jews had lived through the most horrible things human beings can experience. Many of those who survived found themselves distraught and perplexed when they spoke of religion in the context of the inhuman suffering that had been the lot of the Jewish people. That Yehuda's parents could have lived through the tragedy of losing their daughter to the missionaries and still remained such kind and faithful Jews, and the same wonderful mother and father that he and his siblings had known, was now utterly incomprehensible to him often as he thought about it.

It was this kind of spiritual stamina that kept the Jewish people alive and vigorous in the face of all efforts to wipe them off the face of the earth. The words of Abraham occurred to him: Peradventure ten shall be found there. And the reply of the Almighty: I will not destroy it for the ten's sake.

"So long as there are people like our parents, even if their number be minimal, the life of our nation will go on," he thought to himself as he rose the next morning. He felt that he was involved in something that had significance for all Jews, private and individual though this event was. But he didn't have too much time for thinking. At nine o'clock on Monday morning he and Hannah were greeted by the man he had met at the Amsterdam conference almost a year earlier. With the professor were two ladies — his sister, and Yehuda's sister Michalina. The old lady was simply scared of meeting her brother alone.

It would be easy to describe a luridly sentimental scene of brother and sister falling on each other's necks; perhaps they did, too. But that is a scene to be imagined by anyone unwilling to let the two meet in the privacy such an encounter deserves. It is not a moment that can be illustrated by words. Certainly, brother and sister gave themselves no time to consider one another. They were so alike in face and build, so similar in stature, that their relationship could not have been mistaken. The two Italians saw that they could safely disappear for a couple of hours and they left their aunt with her Israeli relatives, sitting around a table on the terrace of a café near the hotel.

Yehuda and Hannah found themselves together with a very pretty old lady who was obviously possessed of a fresh, keen mind and a strong will; she also had a coquettish air that perhaps hid a slight feeling of embarrassment. She was well-groomed and carefully dressed, and her smooth, rosy-cheeked face was devoid of make-up. She was like their father, as Yehuda himself was, except that she had the warm, brown eyes of their mother.

Initially restrained, after a while she began to talk to them as if they had been in close, friendly contact all their lives. Yehuda wanted to know as much about her as he could, but this first conversation brought out little that she had not told them in her letters. Of the first fourteen years of her life she could recall nothing whatsoever. There was nothing in her manner of speech or the expression on her face that could cause her brother and sister-in-law to doubt her sincerity.

Once again she told them what she had so often repeated in her letters — that she had met her father in Breslau two or three years after she had married and would have gone back with him if not for her little son. She seemed to have clung to the memory of this meeting with her father, as if something of importance depended on her not forgetting. (She did not know how her father had found her name and address but on this point her Italian nephew was able to enlighten them later.)

"We wept so much, father and I," she said, "I can't tell you the tears we shed. Father told me then my real name, I hadn't known it before. But Father understood me, he knew I couldn't leave my child." She did not realize what she was implying — that she would not have minded leaving her husband. Of him she spoke very little.

She also revealed that after World War I, she had gone

to Cracow with her brother-in-law in a vain attempt to find someone who belonged to her and to learn whether anything had happened to her father during the war. But the family had left Cracow before the war.

Michalina's nephew, in private conversation with Yehuda and Hannah, confirmed that she had made this search, having heard his father speak of it. They were astounded to learn that Reb Yisrael had somehow found out the name of the man Michalina had married and had learned that this man's family had emigrated to Italy. Apparently, it had not been too hard for him to locate this family since their Polish name stood out in the foreign land. It was to them that Reb Yisrael had addressed his inquiry for his daughter's whereabouts. Her address had been sent to him, thus enabling him to make contact and arrange for the Breslau meeting.

This was an amazing piece of detective work for a modest, studious Chassidic Jew, but he would have done anything in his power to get his daughter back to her people and her faith, no less than to her own family.

Michalina's Italian nephew had been brought up as a Catholic but had grown indifferent to his religion. He was able to explain to Yehuda something of the convents' methodology, and to the Jew it sounded more than faintly reminiscent of the Inquisition. Her nephew also ventured the opinion that by means of hypnosis and other psychological techniques, the nuns had destroyed as many of her early memories as they could, most probably before they sent her from Poland to Belgium. This was later confirmed by physicians in Israel who had dealt with similar cases of brainwashing and who warned that it nearly always damages a part of the brain.

There was irony in the fact that she was led back to her

Jewish family by these relatives of the man she had married. The Church intended such marriages to bind the convert more firmly to Christianity — indeed, by means of her marriage Michalina had been set on the rigid path of Catholic routine. Yet it was marriage that freed her from the fetters of the convent and the surveillance of the nuns, and it was this particular marriage to this particular man that in the long run brought her back to her own family!

These Italian relatives were dissatisfied with the Catholic Church because Michalina's niece had wanted a divorce, but was denied one; they were thus all the more prepared to help their once-Jewish aunt return to her own. But it was pure coincidence that this meeting took place in May, the month of her birthday and the anniversary of her baptism.

Michalina was unhappy with her son at that time, chiefly because he had discarded the Catholicism in which he had been brought up. He had joined the Polish Communist party, which enabled him to divorce his wife and then remarry, events alien to Catholic belief. Therefore, even if her brother hadn't found her, the Catholicism which had cost such a struggle between the mighty Church and the hapless Chassid would have ended with her death. From this one convert, at least, the Church would have gained nothing.

At six o'clock on the evening of that first meeting, Michalina and Yehuda separated for a week. Yehuda and Hannah went on to Yugoslavia and Michalina returned to her niece's house to recover from the emotional turmoil that her carefully controlled exterior had successfully concealed. She was able to discuss the experience with her Italian relatives as she could not have done with her Polish ones, and she was also able to enjoy the feeling of freedom that being abroad for the first time since the outbreak of World War II was giving her. For the first time since she was taken from her father's house in 1899, she had the chance to sit back and be herself.

Being out of Poland definitely released something within her. "As soon as I left the country," she assured her brother, "I knew that I loved you all, my own true family. All my doubts left me."

The Shell

BY THE TIME Yehuda and his wife came back to Italy, ready to spend several weeks with her, Michalina had "come to herself" — or what she thought of as herself.

"I am a Catholic," she said firmly, "I have been so for some sixty years now and I cannot throw it off."

She was so firm on this that any listener would have despaired of effecting a change. She did not yet understand that what had been done to an unwilling, unaware child had to be undone by that same child grown adult. Her Catholicism consisted of faithfully carrying out the prescribed rites in their appointed times, and in never passing a church without entering to utter a few minutes' quiet prayer. Her brother tried to explain something of church history and its pernicious treatment of Jews, from Crusaders to Inquisition to pogroms and blood libels. Her answer shocked him, "Had I remained at home with you all, I would have been gassed like my sisters."

Yehuda, murmuring to himself more than to her, for

her knowledge of the Bible was almost nil, quoted the words of Mordecai to Esther, "Think not that thou shalt escape in the king's house more than all the Jews," adding, "What they did to you in your childhood — was it not the equivalent of death, the death of a Jewish girl to her people?"

Then he took from his breast pocket the photocopy of *Die Welt*, the issue of June 1900, which he had received from his youngest brother in New York, and he quietly asked her to read it. He and Hannah sat watching as her eyes went down the page and her excitement became evident. For the first time she learned the exact details of her fourteenth year. If she had felt stunned when she received the news of having a brother in the world, it was nothing compared to the shock that agitated her entire being now that the full account was laid before her in print. When she finished reading, she gave it back, telling him vehemently, "I don't want this."

"She is so very much bound up with the Catholic Church," Yehuda wrote to his elder brother, Avraham, in Jerusalem, "the problem is very complicated and I feel a heavy responsibility upon me. I am full of tension."

But with the benefit of hindsight one can see that the lock had been broken, and though the door was still tightly shut, it was only a matter of time before it would be opened, not by anyone outside but from within, by her own self. The next morning she came down to breakfast in their hotel and, before putting a bite into her mouth, she begged her brother to give her that newspaper again. This time she kept it.

Heaven alone knows how often she read it through, how many tears she shed over it, for behind the hard, protective shell in which she enveloped herself she was highly sensitive. Yehuda decided not to refer to it again for a while; it was doing its work. It was easy to discern that she was as ignorant of Judaism and Zionism as she was of Christian philosophy, and this gave him the chance to put aside all hurtful matters and keep their talks on an intellectual level. Yehuda had the same enthusiastic nature as his sister, and he was soon able to hold her enthralled while he told her about the great figures of Zionist development.

Michalina had never heard the name Herzl nor had she any idea of the work that Jews were doing in their own country. It was a revelation to her. Apart from that one meeting with her father in Breslau, she had never had any connection with Jews since the day the doors of the convent closed on her. Only once, she remembered, had she passed through a small place in Poland where Jews were living and she had been shocked at what her aristocratic sensitivity considered their uncouth appearance. Her small son had asked her who these people were and why they looked different from the usual village population. She had not known how to answer the child. It did not enter her mind that the separateness of those Jews was forced upon them by the Poles to whom she "belonged."

In fact, in her heart of hearts, she was immensely pleased with her brother. One suspects she may have feared to find him looking like those village Jews with beards and sidecurls and shabby strange clothes. She was vastly relieved, perhaps in something of a snobbish way, to find him so European-looking. She was astonished, too, that her sister-in-law, Hannah, with whom she immediately established good rapport, had left a Western European, enlightened and tolerant country long before

Hitler in order to live in a bleak naked land called Palestine. In her very matter-of-fact way, Hannah gave Michalina a clear picture of the difference in spirit between a Jew finding himself one of a small minority in school and business and a Jew among his own people, building his life in a totally Jewish atmosphere. Michalina hardly understood, however, just what a "totally Jewish atmosphere" meant.

The conversation eventually found its way to another topic. It amazed the old lady when she was told that Jesus was a Jew, a son of this same ancient land where Yehuda and Hannah were living, and that his teachings had their source in the Jewish learning he had imbibed in the most natural way during his childhood and adolescence. She had never been made aware of this before. She was wide-eyed to learn that his mother Mary had probably ignited the oil lamps on Friday nights to usher in the day of rest — *and* on the seventh day of the week, not the first — as the Children of Israel had been commanded. That Jesus had been crucified by the Romans (not by the Jews) in a period of widespread ferment against their rule, and that crucifixion was at no time a feature of Jewish penal law — these were facts that needed some digesting on her part.

Her brother found it necessary to enlighten her on all this right at the beginning, but he would not dwell on it. It was unreasonable to expect her just then to accept this knowledge. He felt easier, naturally, when he could leave the subject and tell her more about Israel. He described in great detail how the Holy Land had been laid waste and neglected, how its soil had become so eroded that its produce was barely enough to support its population, and how the great dream of the return to the land became a reality as a result of the suffering of the Jewish people at the hands of the Christian world and as a result of their faith that God intended them to realize the dream.

"From early in the morning till late at night each day we are with our sister and talking with her," Yehuda wrote to his brothers, "I tell her about Jewish history and about Zionism, but it is a very long road. She sheds tears and has sleepless nights but refuses to discuss anything personal."

Of course, they had only just met. It was impossible at this early stage to talk to her of the ethics of Judaism. His purpose was, first and foremost, to help her feel she belonged to him and the family. With God's help, the rest would follow.

All he could do for the moment was to keep her interested in the affairs of the Jewish people. He told her how they were learning trades and professions which were alien to them in the Diaspora, in order to rebuild the desolate land that had been their home. He told her of his own work as a chemical engineer, and of the factories he had helped plan and establish, which provided work for Israeli Jews and contributed to the development of an export trade for the country. He told her of their younger brother Shaye who was a specialist in seed-growing and in plant diseases, and who had drained his small farmland outside Haifa so that the sandy soil could be refertilized after lying barren for hundreds of years. He gave her a glowing account of their brother Avraham in Jerusalem, whom they affectionately called Avromele. In his youth Avraham had delved into the great philosophies of the world and had corresponded with world-famous philosophers. Like their father, he was a Chassid, with a love of Judaism and Jewish scholarship and an understanding of his fellows that was deep and profound. And Michalina listened, day after day, while subconsciously her pride in her Jewish family grew.

Yehuda also explained to her something of Chassidism. He gave her the history of the man known as the Baal Shem Tov (Master of the Good Name), who believed that devotion to God should be joyous, ecstatic and deeply sincere. He explained how the movement attracted a large following of Jews in the villages of Poland and the Pale, and how it developed into a movement of magnetic power that was still very much alive.

Michalina interrupted him then with a sudden, surprising exclamation, "I remember. There was a *zaddik*, a 'Wonder-Rebbe' from Gora Kalvarya."

Taken aback for a second, Yehuda quickly began to explain to her about these pious leaders of intensely loyal groups of Jews, but her gleam of memory vanished as swiftly as it had come. She complained of a headache and went to lie down.

"She no longer minds that I often call her 'Mechla' instead of the name the nuns gave her," Yehuda wrote home after a few days. "She remembers that father had also called her that."

The Shell Unbroken

MICHALINA'S younger brother, Shaye, who lived near Haifa, and her youngest brother, Leib, from New York, arrived in Trieste to widen the family circle there and to provide Hannah and Yehuda with some much needed relaxation. Shaye was barely a year older than Michalina's own son while Leib was about a year younger. A great many years later, asked what they had been thinking of when they arrived in Trieste, both brothers (though asked separately) gave similar replies: "I was thinking of our parents and their terrible suffering. If only they could have lived to be going towards her as I was. But, in any case, I would have gone anywhere to meet a sister of mine."

The old lady was deeply moved by meeting these brothers who were so much younger than she was; they awakened in her a kind of maternal reaction. Shaye was silver-haired, like herself, though a head taller. He had the gnarled hands of a hard-working farmer and a gentleness of manner that vividly recalled the father she had met over fifty years earlier. But his face was that of their mother whom she could not remember at all. Leib, like his brother Yehuda, resembled their father and herself in features and stature, but he had a kind of pertinacious energy that she attributed to his having lived in America for so long. She was shrewd enough to see that with this brother she would have to tread warily if she was to keep what she thought of as her own soul. The gentleness of the others was disarming and would eventually melt her but this did not occur to her at the time. Together, the brothers complemented one another, to achieve the task they had set for themselves — to right the wicked wrong that had been done to their beloved parents.

With his two brothers there, Yehuda decided he could safely take his wife and go home, leaving Michalina with them for the rest of her stay in Trieste. On the evening before Yehuda's departure, the old lady found herself with her three brothers and her sister-in-law, seated around the table of a private room that Leib had arranged for, with a festive meal set before them. It was a scene she found hard to forget and equally hard to believe both then and later. The conversation fascinated her, yet it seemed dreamlike despite the mundaneness of its topic. For her brothers were indulging in old memories and reminiscences, and nearly all of their sentences began with, "Do you remember...?"

Shaye sat down in an armchair, spreading his fingers on the arms of his chair so that the two middle ones formed a V, something not so easy to do unless it is an old, well-practiced habit. Michalina looked at him, a bit puzzled, till she suddenly looked down at her own hands on the arms of her chair and found them spread in exactly the same way, first and second fingers close together and the third and little one on the other side of the V. It was an old habit of hers, too, and brother and sister, together for the first time in all their lives, looked at one another's hands in astonishment.

They teased her, "Sister, you must have peeped at the Cohanim blessing the people when you were a child, just as we did!"

But as Shaye noticed her face going blank, he quickly took his hands away and said, laughing, "Mother would have said we were spoiling the polish of the wood. She was such a meticulous housewife. Do you remember," he asked his brothers, "our best parlor?" And to his sister he said, "We had one room that was never used! It was very grand, all plush and velvet and polished wood. Mother kept everything in dust covers all the time, and yet she would regularly clean the room although no one ever went in there."

To an Israeli grown accustomed to making use of every inch of space in small dwellings, this memory of an unused room was highly amusing. The Polish "grande dame," of course, couldn't see the joke. It was very natural to have an elegant drawing room and to keep it spick and span.

But Yehuda laughed, too, telling her that the room had been used for betrothals; these occasions were special enough to warrant the room being opened to guests. Shaye took up the theme, speaking as if his sister could participate in these reminiscences, as if they had the same kind of childhood memories, rather than as if he were telling her things that were new to her.

"I think I entered it for the very first time in my life when one of our sisters got engaged," he said. "She sat in state in the best armchair, and at the other side of the room sat her fiancé. He wore the special *streimel* (headgear made of sable) which bridegrooms wear. It was made in points of fur which looked like little tails and I found it very funny. Father, you know, wore a *streimel* of smooth fur."

Hannah hadn't known of these customs, having been born into a non-Chassidic family, and her husband explained that, probably, the bridegroom, being from another town, followed a different group of Chassidim.

The expression on Michalina's face told her brothers that she had no notion of what this was all about. She could not possibly know the importance of marriage to the Jewish way of life, that Jews saw in marriage not merely the coming together of young people but the significance to the whole nation in the building of a new home in Israel.

Leib recalled another incident. "Mother was not allowed in the same room with her betrothed before her own wedding. But she was determined to see what kind of a bridegroom she was going to get. She told us that she stationed herself in a dark corner of the passage and when someone opened the door of the room where her future in-laws were sitting with their son, she managed to get a good peep in."

Michalina was shocked that her parents had not known each other before their marriage. "Do Jewish girls have to marry unknown men?" she asked, trying to keep a critical tone out of her voice.

"Never," her brother answered vehemently. "The times were different — after all, we are talking of more than seventy-five years ago — but nothing was ever arranged without the girl's consent. There was no gallivanting among Jews in that generation. Bride and groom had to be fresh for one another, according to our Jewish laws of *tahara* ("purity"). Our young people could then come to each other without cheap or ugly memories. Father taught us the laws of *tahara* when we were quite young children. One of our elder sisters objected that it was unsuitable for us, but Father thought we should go into life consciously and in full awareness of what intimate life meant. Then we would not behave irresponsibly. Our parents were living examples of the value of these Jewish teachings. Our home was full of respect and affection."

Hannah now entered the conversation. She also had a tale about her mother-in-law to contribute, "Your mother always enjoyed a joke and could take one, too! She was so inordinately proud of you all, and she would always tell me how clever, how wise and talented and upright all her children were. I would let her run on in this way till she had exhausted all her praises and then I used to ask, 'Are all your children musical as well?' Your poor mother! She was very truthful, so she had to admit that this was the one talent they did not possess, they could not sing in tune."

"What! I can't sing?" exclaimed Yehuda in mock dismay. And he began to chant the Chassidic melody "*Schabbes, Schabbes, Schabbes...*," holding his head to one side dramatically. His singing was promptly drowned out by the laughter of his siblings, and their sister felt something that was quite unknown to her, a peacefulness, a tranquility that had a warming quality in it. It was something she had not experienced before; it transfused itself now into her whole being. She wanted this moment to last forever. Any other kind of life seemed too far away to be real. But dawn broke and there had to be a leave-taking as Hannah and Yehuda left for the airport.

So far no one had discussed the future. But later, back in their hotel, Michalina told Leib, "You must understand that I cannot leave my fatherland and go away from my children and give up my religion. I cannot efface sixty years of myself so easily."

"But you believe in life after death, don't you? What about our parents? How will you face them?"

She did not have an answer to this question. To evade it, she turned to Shaye, wanting to know how he had come to leave Europe; with his deep knowledge of the world of nature, he could have become a professor like her son. What urged him to go out to Israel and engage in the physically exhausting work of farming? His answer gave her no chance to evade thought.

"I studied my profession in Holland and then in France," he replied. "After that it was necessary to do a year's practical work and I went to Germany to a large seed firm in Erfurt. This must have been around 1923. Erfurt is in the district of Türingen. In Germany they were very strict about aliens and foreigners even then. Every three months I had to register with the police for a temporary permit to stay there. As soon as the officials saw from my documents that I was a Jew, they would not give me leave to lodge in Türingen for more than three months, so at the end of the period I went over to Prussia to find a lodging there. Each morning I rode in to work in Erfurt and went back to my lodging in Prussia every evening. But the same thing happened there as well, and at the end of three months I had to leave Prussia. I applied for a permit again in Türingen and lodged in Erfurt for the next three months. I got through the year in this way, going from place to place and back as soon as the allotted period was up. And why? Simply because I was a Jew.

There was no other reason for hounding me."

His sister had no reply to this either, and he went on. "Oh well, the Germans got their due in the end; and I live in and work for my own country."

"So do I," she replied, a bit nettled, "Poland is my country."

Leib joined in the conversation again, saying in his emphatic manner, "Now that is interesting. We were all — you too — born in Cracow which was then Austrian. As we all did, you must have left it with an Austrian passport. So I am an American today, Shaye here is Israeli, Yehuda took on Dutch nationality after living many years in Holland — and you are Polish! And we were all born of the same Jewish parents, we have the same grandparents and great-grandparents, going back for generations. Isn't it time to admit that you are a twig of the same stem?"

But it was too early for this. "I married a Pole," she replied, not quite understanding why she should be feeling a bit irritated, yet at the same time rather enjoying this slight friction with a brother, one of many brothers!

Leib was not one to give up easily. He shrugged and said, "And I married a Belgian girl, Shaye's wife was born in England and Yehuda's in Holland. What does all this formal nationality mean to a Jew in a world poisoned by anti-Semitism?"

"Do you think," she asked, determined to hold her ground, "that I didn't see the evil of Hitler when Germany invaded us? I have done a lot for my country, and anti-Semitism had no part in it when they held me in their barracks, those Germans."

Then she told her brothers how she had joined a clandestine group of Polish patriots soon after the invasion of Poland. This group had the misfortune to be arrested by the Germans who had caught them. It had been in the middle of winter. Michalina described how they had all been marched to the railway station in a heavy downpour of rain. In the train that carried them to the labor camp it was so cold that her damp coat froze against the back of her bench.

"When we arrived and it was time to get out, I had to pull myself away by force and a large part of my coat stuck to the back of the seat. In the camp I had to go about with a hole in the back of my coat. Do you know how cold and uncomfortable that was?"

What could her brothers reply? Should they tell this woman, so deprived of her natural heritage, that it had fared worse with the Jews in the other hells of the time, that it had fared so much worse with her own two sisters?

But she was talking on. "I got home when the war ended but nothing was the same any more. Most of my property had gone and there was nothing for me to do but move away from Gola and live with my son in Warsaw."

With that, she was caught up again in the present. Now, too, she would have to go back to Warsaw to her home in her son's apartment. She was not yet clear on just what she would tell her grandchildren about her trip abroad. She would think of that on the way home.

The decision was hers alone. Sixty years of life cannot be erased completely.

Again there was a leave-taking.

Part III
What Next?

THE BROTHERS left Italy within weeks of one another, each in a state of uncertainty and mental turmoil.

Yehuda, so instrumental in having found their sister, felt somewhat baffled that his euphoria had weakened. Was he really disappointed? He wasn't sure what he had expected, but his rather doubting verdict after this first encounter was that "she seems to be vain and superficial."

Leib, back in New York, gave full rein to his feelings as he wrote, "Will she really insist on keeping this faith that was imposed on her, now that she knows exactly what happened to her and how it affected our parents? Perhaps what she wants is the best of both worlds: her brothers and her Catholicism."

Shaye took a different line: "If you make her Catholicism such an important factor in your contact with her, she will be justified in finding it important — and in keeping it so! If we ignore it, she is left with nothing to fight for. After all, we have been privileged to have our sister among us, something not one of us ever dreamed of. How our parents would have rejoiced!"

And Avraham, their elder brother in Jerusalem, placed his faith in the God of Israel, as their father had done, and he quietly prayed that when the Messiah came, as he must, his parents would find their own true daughter again in their first-born child.

The letters circulated between New York, Haifa, Jerusalem and Warsaw with persistent rhythm. But what of Michalina herself? Her first letter from Warsaw, written a day or two after her return, told of her great happiness at having been with her brothers. If only this meeting could have taken place a few years earlier when her father was still alive! When she remembered how short a period had passed since his death, she could lose her self-control and cry aloud for vexation. Her brothers, she thought, possibly didn't realize how deep her feelings were because of her ingrained self-discipline.

She wanted them to know that her first deed yesterday, the day following her return, had been to apply to the Polish authorities for a new passport and exit visa. She told them that if they would send her the necessary invitation she would like to visit them in Israel and perhaps even stay with them for a few months.

Leib, answering this interesting letter, expressed the hope that her visit to Israel implied her taking the one step that would demonstrate her sense of justice. He reminded her of Isaiah 58:7, "Thou shalt not hide thyself from thine own flesh."

Her reply was equally forthright. She loved her grandchildren; they, too, were her own flesh, and it was unthinkable that she should have to break all contact with them. Nor could she (as she had already made clear) suddenly forget the Catholicism and the love of Poland that her soul had kept faith with for more than sixty years. (Interestingly, she took it for granted that as her Catholicism had kept her so completely apart from her own family, so Judaism would keep her separated from her Polish children.)

Leib was filled with indignation. Was their parents' suffering not to be weighed against hers? Did she place her grandchildren on the scales against the mother and father from whom she had been so brutally wrenched? As for Poland, well! Its Jewish citizens had been settled there for generations, yet far from attempting to protect the Jews from the Hitler hordes, the country as a whole had willingly cooperated in sending millions of them to their death in cruelly bestial fashion. In fact, the fine Jewish community of Poland had been virtually wiped out. Was it for love of this brutal country that she was now struggling against the need to do justice to her own flesh and blood and to return to the faith of her fathers? Why so?

"Why so?" was, indeed, a legitimate question. Michalina's brothers realized that it had not been the persuasive power of a religious creed which had made so many conversions and brought tragedy into Jewish homes; it had been the physical might of those in power that was responsible. Michalina, of course, could not have been expected to answer her brother's query — the matter lay far beyond her ken and was not even a strictly religious problem. The notion that children may be stolen from their homes can have nothing ethical about it, whatever the ostensible reason for the deed. Religion is ethics.

"The bond which binds the soul of man to God" is as reasonable a dictionary definition of religion as any. But the forcible conversion of individuals who are already bound in soul to God, as Jews are and have always been, cannot be explained away by that phrase so often used by Christians: "for the salvation of their souls."

It may be that primitive folk living in backward countries where life is governed by superstition, benefit from missionary activity. It brings them not merely schooling and hygiene, but that influence on their conduct which only belief in an invisible, spiritual power can give. Conscience becomes a matter of strictest self-discipline when an all-seeing but unseen eye is constantly observing and judging one's every thought and deed. Neither idolatry nor superstition nor atheism can bring about the same effect on man's conduct.

But nothing of this ever applied to missionary activity among Jews. The Church's directive towards Jews, plainly stated, was: "Jews will practice belief in God in that one way we order them to, or else...," an ideal which is not as deserving of deference as the non-Jewish world would have one think.

Because somewhere in the backyards of time, when princes and rulers came to realize that their own political strength lay in the homogeneity of the community that supported them, it followed that all within their borders must be drawn together in a sameness of formal and ritual conduct. And if at the beginning, the idea of kingship was that of a leader representing God and guiding men in His ways, there came a point in history when kingship demanded obedience as if it were God.

This is the point at which the loftiest and finest of ideals degenerate. Herein lies the fall from that vision of an all-embracing fervor aimed at enhancing the good in the individual and in showing him how to conquer the evil in himself, to an activity that is devoid of humanity; its sole aim is to ensure power for the ruler. In this activity, individuals are but pawns.

The congregation of Capuchin nuns known as the Sisters of St. Felix of Cantalice was the first active Sisterhood in the Russian sector of Poland. It had its Motherhouse in Warsaw. As already noted, this was later set up in Cracow in 1865 by permission of the Emperor Franz Joseph after its suppression and disbandment by the Russian government two years earlier. Poland had revolted against Russia in 1863, and the loyalties of the community of Sisters naturally lay with Poland.

In a personality profile* of the foundress of the congregation, Sophie Truszkowska (known as Sister Marie Angela), the writer describes the latter's desire to "atone to the Divine Majesty in order to obtain Poland's freedom."** The spirit of patriotism had to pervade her community. As many souls as possible were to be imbued with this spirit so that Poland could rise again one day.

Russia, of course, was finding it necessary to keep troublesome Poland suppressed by all means in her power. One of Russia's problems was the great number of Jews with which she found herself saddled as a result of the partitions of Poland. In this matter Czars Alexander III and Nicholas II sought advice from the procurator of the Holy Synod, Constantine Petrovitch Pobyedonostzev. He came up with a simple solution: one third of Russian Jewry would die, one third would leave the coun-

---

*L'*Magnificat* — A centennial record of the Congregation of the Sisters of St. Felix.

**See *Time* magazine, Jan. 4th 1982, "Man of the Year" essay: "During occupation periods, the Catholic Church kept Polish language and culture alive and served as the main bastion of nationalism."

try and the other third "would be completely dissolved in the surrounding population" by conversion.*

The Pale of Settlement pogroms, blood libels, the conscription of very young boys into the Russian army where they were easy targets for conversion — all these were no more than the practical measures required by such a policy. Thus, in nineteenth-century Russia and in occupied Poland the stage was set for widespread missionary activity. Although this was carried out under the banner of "saving souls," neither side (Poles or Russians) lost sight of the goal of raising patriots.

Although perhaps a bit oversimplified, this seems to be the background for the tragedies that cast darkness over the lives of so many Jews well before Hitler arrived on the scene. Religious fanaticism and political power-lust ran along in a mad race, in which the first was eventually overtaken by the other and merged into it. There could never be a place for religious tolerance in a struggle of this nature.

Jews, stateless, often deprived of civil rights and never considered more than second-class subjects, were the easiest of victims. Had the Community of Sisters confined their activities to welfare work among the indigent, as their historians claim, they could never have ensnared girls like Michalina. Her pride in her Polish patriotism attests to the efficacy of their system. Let us not forget that she was not the only one. The Centennial Record of these Sisters tells us drily that "at the Motherhouse on Smolensk Street (in Cracow) they opened a catechumenate for Jewish girls and a free kitchen for poor students."

---

*This is mentioned by James Parkes, Cecil Roth, Howard M. Sachar and others in their histories of the Jews.

No mention is made there of how they got the candidates for this catechumenate, nor why such a place was necessary. It was one aspect of the "great Christian expansion" that characterized the nineteenth century, swallowing up a sizeable number of Jews and Jewesses in its wake.

Michalina could not be expected to come up with such an answer to her brother's question. In part, she was simply scared of change. Nothing in her education had prepared her to accept change as a revivifying element in life. Yet during that short stay in Trieste she had tasted something of a family closeness that she had hungered for since her convent days and that held her magnetized. Her brothers had given her the great gift of family memories. For the best part of that year these memories warmed her like a blazing fire on a wintry day. She felt compelled to enjoy that warmth once more.

Thus towards the end of March 1962 she again took leave of her son, her daughters-in-law, and grandchildren, this time planning to be away for at least three months. She boarded a ship that brought her to the port of Haifa early in April. Her brother Yehuda was there to welcome her and bring her up to his home on Mount Carmel.

Michalina had now to meet the other members of the family, and the curiosity was great on all sides. She was a bit anxious, for this time she was not on neutral soil. Her various visitors saw a pleasant old lady, well into her seventies, with a smile on her lips — and an almost tangible if invisible wall encasing her. Sitting upright in the ladylike way the convent had taught her, her deportment stated, without her uttering a single word, that her fixed intention was to remain the person she had been these past sixty years. "The person I may have been before that is to remain a closed book, to myself as to all of you," — there was no mistaking her adherence to this decision.

Not even her brother Avraham, who made a special trip from Jerusalem to greet her, could change this stance. He was the one she might still have remembered for he had been nine or ten years old when she was taken from her home. Yet, who knew what she was feeling? Although her younger brothers looked European, Avraham could not be mistaken for what he was, a Chassidic Jew. He was a tall man whose snow-white beard was impressive against his sober black suit and hat. He was as dignified a figure as his sister but his dignity came from within. It was not assumed for any purpose of self-defence as hers was. His face was kind, wise, and intelligent, as their father's had been. In fact, she might have been seeing her father again, grown white since Breslau. His eyes had a look in them that she had never seen in any man. Wisdom, understanding, and a warm, gentle humor seemed to combine with a glint of innocent mischief that drew one to him as irresistibly as a babe its mother.

It did not occur to him at that moment that he was a Chassid who never shook hands with a woman; he embraced his sister with all the feeling that welled up in his breast as he called her by the old pet name of her childhood, "Mechla."

Perhaps it was well for her that she had now encased herself so hermetically in the convent walls of her girlhood, as it were; for otherwise her heart must have burst when she greeted this brother. No one could know whether she remembered or recognized him.

Avraham had brought with him the old *Chanuka menora* that their family had used in Cracow. As he took it carefully out of its wrappings, a gleam of memory seemed to light her face. She looked at it, puzzled, saying slowly, "Oh, I remember that. What is it?" It was the same *menora* that her father had lit on the evening before the servant girl took her out for a walk.

Michalina put her hand to her head as if one of her headaches had come on but Avraham sat down at her side and told her in a humorous way about a pair of socks she had once knitted for him when he was a child. She shook her head, disclaiming the memory. Later Avraham told his brothers, "She is a bit *trotzig* (' contrary"), but I'm sure she'll come around, with God's help. She needs time and loving-kindness."

Both were there for her in full measure.

Scales?

GREAT RESTLESSNESS again took hold of Michalina, restrained though she appeared to be. She was unquestionably glad to be with her family in Israel, she felt warm and secure among them, but her thinking was muddled. Israel had not even been a place on the map for her before she met her brothers. She did not understand the world she was in, nor did she know how to keep her footing in it, and it was a bit tragic for her family to observe this. But there was always one thought in her mind: "Can we visit Father's grave?" she asked one day. "I have such a longing to be there."

So Yehuda took time off from work to make the long trip to Jerusalem with Michalina and her sister-in-law, Gissa. Yehuda enjoyed traveling around the country; he loved Israel and was so proud of everything that had been achieved there in so short a time. His enthusiasm was contagious and his sister looked at the passing landscape with lively interest.

Well-taught in his youth by his scholarly father, he was able all along the way to point out places of interest mentioned in the Holy Scriptures, making his companions feel as if they were in the Holy Land of Bible times. However, it soon became apparent that Michalina was not at all familiar with the Pentateuch or the Prophets; her religious knowledge was based on the New Testament alone.

At last, after three hours of driving, they approached their destination. Now the old lady found herself uncomfortably aware of becoming enveloped in an awe-inspiring atmosphere.

The cemetery in Jerusalem lies high on the slopes. As the visitor leaves the traffic-bound road to turn up into the paved pathway leading to the graveyard, he is struck by the silence there. It is almost as if the stark hills that surround the place would quench any need to give vocal vent to feeling. They have the effect of encircling the one who stands there as if that were the only place in the world for a person to be.

At that time, the spring of 1962, the landscape was far less green than it is today. The then almost naked hills that formed the backdrop to the place of everlasting life fashioned an atmosphere of stark severity, harsh and unrelenting. Under the fierce glare of the cloudless skies the white headstones stood out rigidly from every cemented oblong grave, with scarce shadow or hint of green to soften the outline.

Michalina's brother had earlier explained that Avraham would meet them there with eight other men so that they would have the necessary quorum, the *minyan*, for recital of the *Kaddish*. This is the age-old prayer in honor of the dead, that does not mention death at all but renders praise to the Almighty, thus acknowledging His permanence in face of the fleeting nature of human life. At home, the day before, her sister-in-law had taken out the old *Singer's Prayer-book* with its English translation and read this prayer with her, thinking it better that Michalina should know what it was all about. Like a small child, the old lady read it over again in the slow, careful English she had learned so long ago:

"Magnified and sanctified be His great Name in the
world which He created according to His will; May
He establish His Kingdom during your life...."

Then she stopped, declaring excitedly, "But that is what we say in the Lord's prayer: 'Hallowed be Thy Name, Thy Kingdom come, Thy will be done....' It is the same!"

And she was again reminded that Jesus was a Jew and so must himself have declaimed the ancient hymn of praise to God* and then adapted it as the statement containing the one lesson he most wished to drive home to his disciples. Her face took on the blank expression they already knew so well; she was obviously uncomfortable whenever the Jewishness of Jesus was brought home to her. Her sister-in-law noted that "one has to have one's wits about one all the time so as to give her the correct answer to her sudden and unexpected comments." It was quite a strain.

Now, however, Michalina stood at her father's grave-side with an unfathomable look in her brown eyes, and her white head slightly bent in a pious manner as the *Kaddish* was recited. Some quiet seconds passed after the recital

---

Valentine's Jewish Encyclopedia: "From liturgical formulas such as 'Our Father in Heaven,' 'O Lord our God,' 'May His Kingdom Come' etc. the antiquity of certain prayers may be deduced."

while the men dispersed, and then Avraham, in a gentle yet emphatic tone, said that he could hardly have brought his father any better gift than the daughter he had so long wished to have returned to him. She looked up at this, but her sister-in-law broke in quickly with the rejoinder that Father would have wished to have his daughter back as he had known her before she was lost.

Michalina could not help but suddenly have before her eyes the picture of herself as a young matron, when she had told Reb Yisrael that she could not leave her little son and therefore had to return to her husband and her new faith. "My father understood me," she had emphasized to her brothers at their first meeting, but now the tears could not be held back. As the four people walked away from the House of Life, it was obvious that she was suffering and that her whole being was in torment. They drove back to Haifa in almost total silence. It took some days before she gave up the struggle with herself — and her next wish was to visit the holy places in Nazareth!

Tolerant and kind, Yehuda again took a day off to fulfill her wish, joined this time by many members of the family. They came equipped with a large picnic basket; apart from Michalina, no one wanted to give this outing the appearance of a pilgrimage.

Traveling northwards in Israel, one finds oneself in landscape quite different from that encountered in a southward trip such as the road to Jerusalem. The vista in the north is fresh, mellow and smiling, especially in the spring. After the winter rains, the countryside is green and colorful. Though most of the flowers, pale mauve cyclamen and white narcissi, have already been picked or have withered by April, still some bright red anemones poke their inquisitive heads up out of carpets of golden wild chrysanthemums, growing so thickly together along the roadside. But most beautiful in spring are the trees of Israel that come to flower in succession from February to May. The almond tree has lost its delicate, scented flowers, and now the cercis is thick with purple blossom while the bauhenia displays its white and pink fullness amidst a profusion of green leaf. Now the mimosas, which have for weeks been spreading soft feathery golden balls over the roadside, are getting tired, but the jacaranda begins to raise its tall crown of lilac blue flowers against the greyish-white facades of buildings that look garish in the spring light. Very soon, the eritrina blooms in rich red velvet, and all the wild flowers retreat before the dry blasts of the east wind.

So utterly different a countryside from the landscape she was accustomed to in Poland drew all the old lady's interest. Yehuda took his hands from the steering wheel for an instant to wave them in each direction for his sister's gaze, his genial face alight with satisfaction.

"The land is a sleeping beauty come to life again after two thousand years," he told her. "Look at it, just look. You have no idea how arid, how neglected and unloved it looked when we first saw it."

Their brother Shaye, who had come out for the opening of the Hebrew University in 1925 and had stayed a year, confirmed this. So did Hannah, who had also visited the country in those early days and who, after settling, had watched the land blossom as one watches a sickly babe grow round and rosy.

The party thus came into Nazareth in light-hearted mood. They parked the car and walked through the narrow streets with the old donkey ruts running through the middle, and the rather shabby houses that appear to jostle one another as if they had no room. The gently undulating hills in the background beckon to mysterious places in their purple shadows.

By now, Michalina had temporarily forgotten the anguish that she had felt at her father's grave, and she looked about with eagerness. Mary's Well lost something of its glamor for her as she gazed at the ragged, barefooted children and the unfamiliar figures of the people around. Accustomed to the shrines of Poland, she was totally unprepared for the oriental look of this ancient place. But she was assured that this was a genuinely old well, probably two thousand years old, and that it could have been the well from which water was drawn in those days.

What she wanted to visit, however, was the Basilica of Annunciation. Although the old lady spoke little, her feeling was that there she would be able to come to grips with herself and her problem. If there was an Almighty Power in the world Who had compassion on her, it would be in that place, the largest Catholic church, that she would be given her sign and would know which way to go. Her companions made no comment to her, nor did they speak of her wish amongst themselves, they simply asked the way and brought her there.

And perhaps it was there that she got her sign: the church was closed for repairs and would not reopen for several weeks. Her face fell and her brother led her to a nearby bench where she sat down lifelessly and refused to open her mouth or let anyone talk to her. She looked as though everything dear in life had been taken from her, the picture of despair.

After a time, the family suggested moving on. They could go on to Tiberias, see Capernaum, Migdal. She would have none of it. She showed interest in nothing.

The church, the holy church of her lord, was closed to her and the sun had gone down. With the heavy tread of a very tired old lady, she walked listlessly back to the car for the drive to Haifa. The gates of the convent had been similarly closed to her father when she had been behind them, and he had so yearned to see her. She was very conscious that day of a certain pattern of history.

Strange World

BUT THEN Passover came upon the land, and a normally exuberant Israel was caught up in an overwhelming ecstasy of preparation, as it is perennially. This Feast of Freedom has always been beloved by Jews, but has now a particular significance for a generation that has itself "been delivered from Egypt." From the smallest outlying settlements to the larger towns, in village, outpost, and hamlet, there is a fussing and a hustling and a bustling as if the very millennium were on the threshold. There is not a person on the streets for weeks in advance who is not struggling with some heavy, ungainly parcel or a full and bulky shopping bag, and there is nothing so hard as to squeeze one's way onto a bus amidst the package-laden commuters.

For Michalina, this was an entirely new experience. If she had seen anything similar in Cracow during the first thirteen years of her life, nothing of it remained in her memory. It did not occur to her to wonder what kind of

Pesach her parents had spent that year of 1900 when she was missing at the table and they had little hope of getting her back. But her brothers pictured the scene in their mind's eye as often as they looked at her, caught up like any Jewess in the highly infectious excitement of the general atmosphere. Nazareth, they noticed, was receding into the twilight.

As she got involved in helping her hosts with the preparations, she not only regained her old placid self, she almost turned into the Jewish housewife. While occupied in folding napkins and giving a last polish to glasses, she amused those around her with stories about her acquaintances in Poland, and soon had them laughing at the tale of a woman friend who disliked her husband's drinking habits. Whenever the poor man was offered a drink, his wife would quickly say, "My husband gratefully declines."

"Mine doesn't," said Hannah, laughing as Yehuda allowed himself a small glassful of brandy after the morning's exertions. Michalina, in a spirit of saucy coquetry, picked up a glass and declared, "Well, now that Yehuda has drunk to his own health, let us drink to ours!"

She was sister, she was aunt and great-aunt, she was an integral member of a clannish Jewish family, she had lived among them all her life — so it seemed!

When *seder* night arrived and she took her seat at the long, beautifully decked table she was an eager and animated woman, far from that walled-in Polish lady they had greeted so formally just a few short weeks back. There were so many little ones about and she loved children, forgetting herself and her restraint in their company. How tremendously she enjoyed having five-year-old Ruthie teach her some Hebrew words and how diligently she tried to repeat the strange sounds.

The chatter died down at last, and everyone settled in to the matter on hand, opening the *Haggada* that lay at each place. For Michalina they had found one with a German translation and boldly etched illustrations so that she could understand the text and amuse herself with the pictures.

The blessing was made, the verse on the Bread of Affliction recited, the Four Questions were asked and tunefully answered, and the service was in full and fluent swing, each participant taking turns to read or chant the ancient account of Egyptian bondage, while some of the adults round the table quietly recalled some particular aspect of a more modern and inhuman bondage.

From time to time one of her brothers would look at her and wonder what was going on in her mind. Was this no more than a feast to her, a family occasion, or did it awaken anything deeper in her breast? Was it really possible that the *matza* was now totally strange and new to her?

But she was reading quietly to herself, and the person sitting next to her noticed that she was fully concentrated on the printed page, and, paying closer attention, discovered that she was not looking at the translation at all; this daughter of Israel was reading the Hebrew, murmuring it to herself in the Ashkenazi accent she had been taught in her childhood. In loud surprise, this person exclaimed, "But, Mechla, you are reading Hebrew, you can read it better than I can!"

And, of course, as the eyes of the whole company turned upon her, her face went blank again. She looked helplessly at the Hebrew page, found it a mass of printed signs that were quite unintelligible, and put her hand to her forehead as if it were paining her. Yehuda quickly went on with the service but she turned to the translation, soon lost interest and was unable to follow any more. She found herself alone, in a world that was not hers.

To bring her back, so to speak, someone related a Chassidic folk-tale: the Rabbi of Berditschev heard from some merchants that there was considerable activity in smuggling, and he said, "See, the king has many soldiers and officers but hasn't the power to halt the smuggling. The God of Israel has no army, yet no one dreams of smuggling *chametz* (leavened bread) into their homes during *Pesach*. Such a nation is Israel!"

Michalina smiled politely and asked about the *matza* and how it was made. So they told her another tale, this time about Rabbi Meir Margulis who, just before *Pesach*, was walking along in the mud near the river, carrying a large pitcher. He was met by a *maggid* (an itinerant preacher) who was riding in a wagon and who stopped to ask why Rabbi Meir was walking in the mud. Explained the latter: the *mitzva* of drawing water for the baking of the *matza* comes only once a year, and he thought it unseemly to share this *mitzva* with a horse. Thereupon, the *maggid*, too, descended from his wagon and walked along with Rabbi Meir in the mud.

To many of the youngsters there, these were tales of a world unknown to them. They had never realized how deep and strong an influence Judaism had exerted on Jews in their daily lives during the Exile. But Michalina's eyes seemed too bright of a sudden. Was it the glitter of a tear?

When her brother Avraham came from Jerusalem to visit her again after the festival, he found her "greatly improved"; she was softer, less contrary. She recalled various Yiddish expressions and asked what they meant, she pinned on to her dress a brooch Avraham had brought her that had belonged to their mother, expressing her pleasure in having it. Her ambivalent attitude towards her mother had not yet found utterance, or perhaps she had not yet visualized her mother as a real person. Possibly the mere fact of living in such close contact with her very Jewish relatives in their own home was as much as her mind could cope with for the time being.

Her sister-in-law, Gissa, reported to Leib in New York:
> She has this terrible fear that because of her participation in our life here, she will have to burn in hellfire. This is such an un-Jewish notion. And yet, if she knew herself to be a truly loyal Christian she would not have this fear, so that, painful as it is to note, it may be a hopeful sign.

But still, it seemed to her family that, try as they might, something of a distressful nature was always underfoot to trip them up, even in ways that seemed quite irrelevant. The film *Exodus* was showing in Haifa one week and Yehuda suggested that she be taken to see it; it could make the idea of the Return vivid and comprehensible to her just then when the significance of *Pesach* had been so carefully explained. It could give her a view of what her own people had gone through, that no theoretical history could. Therefore, one bright afternoon, Michalina went to the cinema, joined by Gissa and a young niece. She enjoyed seeing the film, even getting caught up in it in the enthusiastic spirit that was part of her nature.

In the interval which always interrupts the action and brings an audience down to earth again, she felt that she would like to do something for her hosts to show her gratitude. She took out a coin, a woefully small one, and asked her niece Talma to buy ices for the three of them. Having been in the country for so short a time and hardly ever having been out on her own, she had no idea of prices. Gissa motioned to the child to say nothing but to go out with all those thronging the aisles. A few minutes later, Gissa excused herself, quickly went out to find Talma and give her enough money for the ices before she returned to the hall.

But the child had been entrusted with too difficult a mission for her years. She distributed the ices — and then poured some change into Gissa's lap. The latter was too embarrassed to know what to do on the spur of the moment. To tell her guest that her coin had been insufficient would be to hurt her, and yet it looked as if Gissa were pocketing change that did not belong to her. On the other hand, had she given the change to Michalina, she would soon have noticed that there were a few coins among it equivalent to the one she had given Talma. The dimming lights saved the situation, but there was an uncomfortable feeling between the two women on the way home, and Gissa could not easily get over her embarrassment. The idea that Michalina must surely have thought her a cheat, and that perhaps she was thinking "a Jewish cheat," nagged at her mind relentlessly. She didn't bother to ask later what comment the old lady had made about the film or how it had affected her.

The whole period was one of hypersensitivity on all sides. When that first month came to an end, Shaye and Gissa invited her to stay with them for a time, in this way affording Yehuda and Hannah some relief from the strain. Michalina felt very comfortable on the small farm outside Haifa, recalling that her husband had been an agricultural engineer and this aspect of life was familiar to her.

But a farm in the young Israel of 1962 was not one in Poland. In the early thirties, her brother Shaye had undertaken to turn a few acres of scorched sand dunes into arable soil. Thirty years of unremitting labor had made the place unrecognizable. Gay geraniums bordered a path between green, peaceful lawns, leading to a long, low, flat-roofed farmhouse, hiding itself modestly in a profusion of greenery. Tall palms reached to heaven, giving protection from wind, while the shiny, thick leaves of the rubber plant absorbed much of the sun's heat.

Surrounded by a variety of cactus plants, tall and spiky or squat and hairy, a large birdhouse sheltered a number of lovebirds, green, blue, and yellow, that twittered incessantly and afforded both pleasure and instruction to the children growing up in this free environment. A few geese quarreled in their pen and a turkey insisted on flying over the hedge as often as it could so that the children might bring it back.

Behind the house grew the mulberry trees and, nearby, citrus trees spread their hospitable boughs while shrubs and plants of every possible kind found a home in the welcoming earth.

The place so clearly illustrated the love of the Jew for his own home and what it meant for him to be free, undisturbed by the inimical forces of repression. Transforming dunes into such a green paradise meant rising every morning well before dawn to dig and till before the heat became uncomfortable. It meant a day's work in town for the sustenance of the family, it meant coming home not to rest but to go out in the comparative cool of the evening and lovingly pick off the dead leaves, snails, and the weeds that demanded their survival, too, in the freshly nourished soil. It meant unceasing care, not in the plodding way of a peasant following the earthbound ways of generations of forebears, but with the reflective devotion, the keen observation that a mother would give a very fragile child after long years of waiting to conceive.

It meant all this and more. Nothing was taken for granted, everything had to be marked, noted, discussed for the benefit of all those Jews so new to this type of life. There were consultations and meetings of the local council late at night when it was too dark to do any more physical work, advice to be given and taken by puzzled neighbors coming in at all times. There were arguments on methods, criticism of organization, greater attempts at coördination, liaison with authorities — in brief, it all left no time for self.

When Michalina saw her younger brother fall asleep in his chair after such days, she no longer asked why "he went in for such a hard life"; she knew the answer. He and his fellows had no fear that their children would be abducted by missionaries and lost to them. Here the Jew could protect his young and defend his family. In its own country, the Jewish nation had a future.

"That despicable thing, that servant girl," she was heard to murmur.

"Come, Mechla," called her sister-in-law, "let's go for a walk in the village."

"Take her through the wood," said Shaye, "show her the trees we planted from seed thirty years ago." He added: "I remember how Father taught us when we learned Talmud together that there is no more genuine sign that Redemption is near than the sight of groves in Eretz Yisrael" (*Sanhedrin* 98a).

But Gissa, townswoman, wanted to show off the asphalt road newly laid down in the village. "For years and years," she said, "we have been treading in the sand, and this new road cost each of us so much money. I want to enjoy walking on it."

And this, too, was a mistake. The new road led straight to a small synagogue at the end of the village. As they walked along, Gissa savoring so contentedly the road under her feet, she soon became aware that Michalina was clutching her arm as though suddenly scared. Not understanding why, there being neither horse nor cow, neither turkey-cock nor goose in their way, Gissa patted the hand that lay on her arm and continued to point out things of interest along the way, a new barn or shed here, a new outbuilding to the dairy there. But the old lady had her eyes fixed on the unmistakable building with its rooftop *menora* at the end of the road, and she began to tremble uncontrollably.

As they approached it, she urged Gissa to go a little more quickly, but then she wanted to turn and go home. She was tired. So they turned back and very gradually the trembling ceased and the nervous, hurried step began to slow down. Thereafter she asked to go through the wood, saying she liked the feel of earth under her feet.

Hellfire

SOON AFTER Michalina's capricious flight from the synagogue precincts, her brother Yehuda came out to the farm to visit her, bringing with him two stand-up photographs of their parents. Beaming, he set these up on the little table at her bedside so that she could see them first thing in the morning and have the feeling she was at last safely home. It worked out differently, however.

Going into the room in the morning to dust and make the bed, Gissa found the photo of Reb Yisrael upright as Yehuda had placed it, but that of their mother was lying face down. The first day she thought this was an accident and stood the picture up. But the next day and the next and, indeed, whenever she went into her sister-in-law's room, she found her mother's photo on its face. Obviously, it was a deliberate action, and Gissa took an early opportunity to ask Michalina about it. Hiding her embarrassment under a tone of flippancy, the old lady said, yes, she had intended to pick some flowers to put by the photo. "No," said Gissa very firmly, "you will not." At this, Michalina was startled out of her pose of indifference. "Why not?" she asked. "Because there is no point in placing flowers with a disloyal heart." "But I cannot recall my mother or anything about her. Is that disloyal? Not to remember?"

Gissa then felt that she had to be forthright, it was useless to beat around the bush. "You just can't bear to look at your mother's face, so you turn the picture over. But you know she is your mother. You know she bore you, cherished you, and then lost you. And you know how she lost you — to those who have never been friends of our people, the missionaries. You know what plain justice demands. But you can't face up to it."

Michalina looked up in wonder at her sister-in-law's unwonted severity, but Gissa, having taken the plunge, would not draw back and went on, "You know today that when they told you you were an orphan, they lied to you. Actually you have always known it since the day you spoke with your father in Breslau, all those years ago. Perhaps you were helpless then, but you are not now."

The old lady kept silent, hanging her head a bit. Gissa began to fear that she really had been too severe. The truth was, though, that Gissa's rebuke bore little weight against indoctrination carried out at the impressionable age of fourteen; the anguish this caused Michalina in her old age was too great for her to deserve castigation, irritating though her obstinacy seemed.

Deeper insight, however, requires digression into a field seldom trodden by Jews. The Record of the Felician Sisters shows that their whole soul and being was invested in the "Immaculate Heart of Mary." Their ideal — termed by their historian the "Marian ideal" — was the spirit of reparation to be developed by mortification and penance. The exercise of this penance included control of the "passions, emotions, affections and memory, imagination, reasoning and will." Furthermore, in order to "revive the spirit of reparation of the community" the Sisters were charged with undertaking this task (of mortification) at the risk of being "ridiculed by the world and even by souls consecrated to God." The nuns imbued with this spirit were the nuns who educated the fourteen-year-old Michalina.

At the solemn moments of their reception, their first profession and the day of perpetual vows, the Sisters are offered to "Our Lady" and declare that "they choose the Mother of their Lord Jesus as their *own* Mother and Lady, and entrust their vows and promises to her Immaculate Heart." One may respect native Christian women whose renunciation of the world in this way is made in sincere nobility of soul, according to their lights. But forcibly imposing it on Jewish girls is another matter.

So if it was unfair to expect Michalina to perceive or explain the cause of her Polish patriotism, much less could one demand that she analyze her attitude to her natural mother and admit that she should feel otherwise than she had been taught. She had been indoctrinated by those to whom *Matka Boska* (Polish for "Mother of God") was the beginning and the end of life as well as its content. The adolescent girl had been permeated with this spirit through and through.

In fact, when they prepared her for baptism, their original intention had been to make her a nun, too, so that apart from weaning her away from her natural affections in order to train her for their purposes, the very training itself entailed the suppression of both affection and memory. Her own rebelliousness and her parents' persistent attempts to regain her had finally saved the young Michalina from the cloister and had enabled her to enjoy the normal affections of her own motherhood, but memory was not so easily restored.

She had been made to choose Mary "as her own Mother and Lady." Against all "reasoning and will" she simply "knew" that were she to give up Mary she would burn in hellfire for everlasting. This idea had been deeply implanted in her, and she was terribly afraid of burning. One had the feeling that she was practically bound to the stake in a revived auto-da-fè. It was a fate she so awfully dreaded that compassion was the only possible response, but it was a response no one dared to demonstrate.

To the outsider it may seem harsh that her family obliged her to confront the situation. Yet naturally they could not forget that this choice of a mother had not been taken of her own free will. Her brothers could never forget the Friday nights in their childhood home. Their mother would look around at her family and a sadness would shadow her face as she prepared to bless the candles. When she took her hands away from her face, her eyes invariably had the glitter of tears in them. Yet she never gave her family a hint of the grief that tore at her heart. Mary had been forced upon Michalina by unfair means and even the outsider can hardly declare such coercion to be less than heartless.

In relating the "affair of the photographs" to the family, Gissa defined it as a case of "Honor thy father and thy mother" at one end of the pole, and "Woman, what have I to do with thee?"* at the other end. There was no recon-

*St. John 2:4.

ciling the two attitudes. The Jew "believes with perfect faith that to the Creator ... and to Him alone it is right to pray and that it is not right to pray to any other being besides Him."* There is also the Jewish credo that "there will be resurrection of the dead at the time when it shall please the Creator...." At such a time Michalina should be able to face her parents in the knowledge that she had honored them as the commandments exhort Jews to do.

Whether each of the brothers was a rigidly observant Jew or not, they were all absolutely faithful to the spirit of their parents and their Judaism, and could not condone action that rejected this spirit. Returning, heart and soul, to her own people and their way of life was the only way that Michalina could honor her father and mother.

"But I am afraid," she whispered, "my soul will burn in hell; that is something I cannot bear. It would be too dreadful."

"And that is something I cannot understand," replied Gissa. "I am sure that you have always been a good person, helpful, kind, and honest. Why then should you have to burn in hell?"

"But we are all sinners," rejoined this poor old lady, "we are born in sin."

Gissa shook her head, then quoted softly, "'The soul that Thou hast given me is pure because Thou hast created it.' Your father must have taught you that when you were still at home. Why can't you accept it?"

Once more, it was unfair to expect an answer. The foundress of the Congregation of Felician Sisters had declared that "Hell devours so many souls" and had given

---

* "The Thirteen Articles of Faith," Maimonides.

assurance that Mary is the mother of all and had promised that since she had been so appointed, none of her children should perish. Who was Michalina to contradict these teachings? They had been impressed upon her by every possible means.

This old lady had lost her husband and her daughter to illness, had seen her son lose his soul to Communism, and had lost her property in war. It had been her faith in Mary's love that had sustained her through all this. How *should* she now give it up?

Gissa told her bluntly, "You know, you cannot have both Mary and the mother who bore you and wept for you with her last breath."

Very sadly, very sincerely, and in a very low tone, Michalina replied, "I know. I know that I must grapple with this problem."

The Gleam of Hope

IT WAS NOT at all helpful that at this time — when she had been in Israel for just over a month — letters from Poland began to arrive for her. It was easy to see from whom these letters came. If she folded up the pages with an air of quiet pride and then went about rather thoughtful and quiet, the letter had come from her son or grandchildren. After a day or two she would tell the family about these children, what they were doing and how they were building up their careers. She was immensely fond of them. But if she bowed her head and was depressed and crept around the house without asking for company, then the letter had come from her divorced daughter-in-law who exhorted Michalina not to forget her prayers to Mary, and scolded her for not going to church or confession. Too many such letters began to arrive and, of course, their effect on her was distressing.

Still, it did happen once that the family felt luck to be on their side. She got a letter from a niece or cousin of her deceased husband, which sent her running to Gissa so that she could read it aloud for, as she said, "It is a wonderful letter, you must feel it was written by someone with understanding."

Her relative had written:

> I would advise you to stay in Israel. It is apparent that you are happy with your family there, that you are loved and well-treated. As for the question of religion, don't let it bother you. Even the Pope said recently that there is only one God and He is for all.

It was ironic that the Pope, however unwittingly, had a hand in tipping the scales, if ever so slightly in favor of this "convert's" return to her folk and their faith.

With this letter in mind, her brothers thought that it might be the time for Michalina to visit her mother's grave as she had visited their father's. So again Yehuda took a day off and with Gissa and his sister drove off early one morning. Their mother had found her last resting-place in the cemetery near Tel Aviv.

Michalina's mood that day was not the best and Yehuda decided to give the trip the more pleasant air of an excursion. Accordingly, he drove up to Zichron Ya'acov, a pretty, sleepy little town on the Carmel hills with something of an old-world atmosphere. For the best part of an hour they wandered through the beautiful park of the Baron and stood for a few minutes by his tomb while Yehuda told his sister of the Baron's work on behalf of his people. Yehuda tried so hard to lighten the atmosphere and change her mood, telling her, as they walked back to the car, the old joke about the very poor couple who came to visit the place in a spirit of homage. The man gazed long and earnestly at the marble mausoleum, then turned and told his wife, "You see, Chaya, this is the way to live!"

Michalina hardly smiled. She was determined to be unhappy. Or was she controlling her emotions, doing penance for her impulsive reaction to her niece's letter?

They came into Tel Aviv around noon and she asked if she could have something to eat before going to the cemetery, since she had not taken much breakfast that morning. Her brother was only too glad to drive to a pleasant little restaurant and to order for her the food he knew she most enjoyed. But no sooner had the waiter left their table than she complained of a headache and said she couldn't eat anything.

Yehuda felt helpless to deal with the situation and began to feel irritated, especially after she expressed a wish to return to Haifa. This was too much and Gissa put her foot down. They had come this far for a purpose and there was no point in going home without achieving it. She went to find a pharmacist and buy some aspirin, suggesting that meanwhile a cup of strong coffee would do the old lady good.

The aspirin may have helped the headache but the food was left untouched. Michalina looked on unconcernedly while the bill was being paid, and in silence the party went out to the cemetery.

What was she afraid of? It was impossible to tell. Why had she trembled and fled from the synagogue a week or so before? Vague, subconscious memories can be highly disturbing, all the more so since one cannot nail them down. Had it to do with those early days when she had cried for her mother and no mother had come because, unknown to her, the nuns had not allowed it? Such memories were too deeply buried, and all she was aware of was a nameless fear and reluctance.

This time there was no *minyan* and no reading of the

Kaddish. Her brothers had agreed that privacy was the best policy on this occasion. But Michalina stood there at the graveside with a wooden countenance, not even looking down at the grave, as if all this had nothing to do with her. Gissa, knowing how much all the brothers revered their mother, could feel just how Yehuda must have been reacting with this very sullen sister at his side, and she kept silent.

All three walked back to the car, dejected. However, once they were outside Tel Aviv on the road to Haifa, Michalina's mood changed again, or perhaps she was feeling that it was her duty to cheer her companions up; she became once more the pleasant sister with a fund of humorous small talk to break the silence. No mention of the past hour was made — it was too painful. Her sudden changes of mood were hard to take.

Nevertheless, after that day, the photograph of her mother stood upright all the time, side by side with that of her father, and one day Gissa found a little vase of fresh flowers beside it. The flowers were changed daily, Michalina going out into the garden to pick them with the utmost care and arrange them lovingly with an eye to mixture of color and kind. She was so sincere, so reverent in this little task that at last Gissa had the courage to ask her if she could recall something of her mother.

"I spend hours and nights thinking about it," Michalina admitted, "but the whole picture is gone from me. I can recall nothing." She paused, then added more vigorously, "But I do know how she must have suffered. I remember when my daughter died. It was so terrible. How could the church have taken me like that! It was a cruel thing to do."

Would there be a change of heart? Could there be?

The Impossible

APPARENTLY, there could be. It
is easy to make random guesses about
people's conduct and to justify such guesses by means of
pseudo-psychological interpretations. But how close to
the truth can one get?

In the summer of 1960 Michalina had stated very firmly
to her brothers, "For sixty years I have been a Catholic
and shall die in this faith; also I am a Pole and have done
very much for my fatherland. These two points are inseparable from me." And for two years these two points were
the only cause of disagreement between the brothers and
their sister, whether in the correspondence prior to their
meeting or in their conversations after it. But the time
was now drawing near for her visa to expire — she had
already overstayed her three-month visit. It seemed as if
she could not bear to tear herself away, but now she had to
come to a decision. Her brothers, reluctantly resigning
themselves to her obduracy on the question of her faith,
advised her to get ready to return to her son in Warsaw so

that she would not lose her rights as a Polish citizen. She had spent her time in Israel with each of her brothers alternately, and now in August she was again staying with Shaye and Gissa. The whole family had been watching and hoping for a sign that she was ready to "return," and Hannah had recently thought that perhaps the old lady was becoming less enthusiastic about her Catholicism. Michalina would often wonder aloud how the Church could possibly have stolen a child from her parents.

"Well, Mechla," said Gissa one morning, "so we shall soon be losing you."

"I would like to stay here with you all," was the astounding reply, spoken quietly, perhaps a bit timidly, "but I cannot go back and forth between you like a football. If I have only a short time to live, that wouldn't matter, but if there are still some years of life in store for me, what then? What would my brothers do with me?"

It has come so quietly, so naturally, that Gissa replied matter-of-factly, as if nothing very special had been said, "There are some very pleasant Senior Citizens' Homes in the neighborhood." But then she thought she hadn't heard properly. "Do you mean you would really like to stay here? Do you know what that implies?"

"Yes," the other answered quite calmly. She had obviously come to a well thought-out decision. "I was born Jewish and so I suppose I must be Jewish." Watching her sister-in-law's face as she made this astonishing declaration, Michalina continued as if she had actually heard the unspoken thought, "I have studied my prayer-book and found a prayer that makes no mention of the Trinity but addresses itself to God alone. I am too old to learn new forms and I am used to saying my prayers morning and night. From now on, I shall use this prayer that I have found and no other."

What must it have cost her?

It was unbelievable and accepted by the family with awe rather than with jubilation. The sacrifice she was making was enormous, beyond all comprehension. Such a step meant first of all that she was likely never to see her son or grandchildren again. It was hardly probable that they would come to Israel and she certainly could not go to Poland again. This final separation from her loved ones — and they were the only ones of her own flesh and blood that she had had since the day she was abducted — would cause her more pain than anything else, her trained Christian stoicism notwithstanding. It also meant that at her advanced age, she would have to accept a way of life unlike anything she had ever consciously known; for the second time, she would "be made over." From being a Polish lady, treated with the scrupulous respect due to age, sex, deportment, and the fact of having been honored by her country, she would become merely an old woman in a Senior Citizens' Home in a country that in 1962 was still very youthful, with youth's uncaring attitude to age.

Every immigrant has to be prepared for a modicum of change that requires the effort of adaptation, but Michalina was not just "an immigrant" — her starting-off point differed too greatly, even in trivialities. A great many of her meals would be taken in the common dining room of the Home where her dainty, polished table manners and habits would contrast, often glaringly so, with those of people of entirely different background and upbringing. Instead of indulging in well-bred small talk across the tea table, she was more likely to find herself bombarded by heated discussions on the part of companions who considered themselves politicians, fully equipped to take over the government of the country and conduct its foreign and economic affairs. Was her mind still fresh enough to enjoy such freedom of thought or would it shock and frighten her after years under Communist rule?

Then again, she would often hear castigation of her beloved Poland from those who had suffered from its anti-Semitism. How would she react to that? She would be unable to share her own memories and experiences with Jews who, even before their immigration to Israel, had spent much of their time amongst Jews, whether in *shtetel*, ghetto, or the more Jewish quarters of big cities.

There was but a single common memory to which she could respond. When mention of the Holocaust came up, she could say that she, too, had lost two sisters in the gas chambers. What a fact to bind her to her own! Eichmann had been given his deserts in Israel that June and her attitude to this was as natural as that of any Jew.

And even then, the sum total of the change she was about to make was far wider, far greater, involving far more than a change of scene and social climate. She had to adjust to the physical climate itself. The bright sunshine, the glare of the almost cloudless blue skies for a great part of the year, the subtropical heat of summer with its dry, desert east winds, and the fierce downpours of rain in the short winter, the near lack of real autumnal or spring weather to cushion the changes — her body had known none of these. Even the fruits and vegetables, the gastronomical ways of this warm, Mediterranean country had little in common with those of Poland. But this was the least of it; her spartan, convent upbringing would stand her in good stead here. Indeed, it seldom occurred to her that she had the right to dislike what was set before her.

Her family, however, was mainly concerned about her

psychic well-being amidst the Israeli rush of life. Michalina could hardly have realized what it would mean to her never again to wake on Sunday mornings to the chime of church bells, but to see the day pass as an ordinary workday. On the other hand, she would find no shops open on Saturday (to her simply the day after Friday), neither bank nor post office nor hairdresser. Her whole weekly routine would have to be realigned. Could she do this at seventy-six and remain unconfused?

Actually, it was far easier to do in Israel than it would have been had she gone back to live with a branch of her Jewish family anywhere else in the world. There the non-Jewish life of the place would have exerted its own pull. For unless she meticulously examined a calendar that might have been sent to her from Warsaw, nothing in the daily life of Israel, Orthodox or secular, would mark out for her the Saints' Days and the Feasts she had been wont to observe.

Alone with herself during the long nights, would she not suffer agonies of remorse and fear of punishment if she suddenly awoke to the awareness that it was Lent, for instance, and she should not have eaten meat that day, or that she should have been taking her festively clad granddaughters to offer special prayers?

Her grandchildren! Would the thought of them not cloud her eyes again and again? And how should she not think of them, this woman who, for all her self-imposed, iron restraint, was so full of affection and so in need of it?

Furthermore, her family could not help wondering whether she would be able to take a walk near the synagogue and not hasten her steps to flee as she had done the first time. Could she observe bearded Jews in their distinctive caftans and headgear and not draw back — as she had once related she'd done when driving through a small village in Poland? But she had accepted her brother Avromele without comment on his appearance, indeed with love and joy.

And what about the Jewish Sabbath, so different from the Polish Sunday — could she take part in that without being aware of any separateness? She was too old now to feel at home among the part of the population that spends Shabbath in prayer and in reading the Scriptures. But at the other end of the scale, she was also too old to be comfortable with those who put on their sloppiest clothes for joyrides and picnics. Between these two extremes could her feeling of Jewishness become such that she could yet feel and enjoy the distinctiveness of the Shabbath with its unfailing air of calm and withdrawal from the weekday tempo? It would be a pity for her to become just an automaton in the Israeli way of life.

And how would she manage, with her fear-trained habits, if she felt the need to relieve her conscience of any peccadilloes? She could not go to Mass or to the Confessional. In Judaism the individual is accountable directly to God for his or her misdeeds.

After some thought and consultation amongst themselves, the family came to the conclusion that nothing should be done which could be interpreted as coercion. They had explained everything to her, but refused to see themselves as missionaries. If she returned to her non-Jewish Polish family, her Jewish relatives would continue to keep in touch with her and perhaps even see her in Europe if that were possible. They were now on very good terms with her late husband's relatives in Italy and arrangements could probably be made. In fact, it had been the first time in her life that Michalina had seen Jews and non-Jews comfortably together, as was the case in Italy the year before, and this had also left its impression on her.

On the other hand, if she really desired to make her home in Israel and to live as a Jewess among Jews, her brothers would see to it that she got a pleasant room in a Senior Citizens' Home within walking distance of Yehuda's house. But they would not help her to complete all the formalities involved. She alone would have to take care of these; it would have to be entirely of her own free will.

Her family felt that to a person brought up in Christianity all such points would be problems and it did not seem possible that Michalina could make such a decision. And yet she did.

Was it a mere sense of rectitude? Or was it her instinctive feeling of belonging to the family, her desire not to be separated again? Did she feel she owed it to her parents' memory to return? Or had she come to understand what it was in herself that had sent her out traveling and searching in the wake of a strange yearning as soon as she was free of the convent? Probably it was a combination of all these factors; it was more than likely that she could not have clearly defined her own reasons for the hard-won decision. Undoubtedly, she was influenced by the shock and revulsion she felt over the Church's deception of her and the evil it had done to her parents.

It was hard to say whether her fears about burning in the afterlife had been quieted, but she did have one reservation about staying in Israel: she could not bear the idea of being wrapped in a shroud and buried directly in the ground, dust to dust. Her brothers had explained to her clearly that her decision to consider herself Jewish and remain with them would entail Jewish burial. She begged very hard for a coffin, no matter how plain. It was her only wish, poor woman!

Her brother, Avraham, having learned about her terrible fear of burning, had sat down with her during his most recent visit to Haifa and had explained something of the teachings of the Rabbi of Gur: "If a person has a fear of anything except the Creator, he is in some degree an idolator. For to fear is to offer worship to the thing feared, and this form of worship may be offered only to the Almighty."

This she grasped with the gratitude of a troubled person being helped and comforted. In response to her talk of sin, he told her, "Kindness and truth cause sin to be forgiven." This brother, so clever, learned, and good, found the right words to put her fears at rest so that, at last, she could by herself, go downtown to the government offices to request application forms for a tourist who wanted to become an immigrant.

She brought these forms to Gissa for help in filling them out. Putting entirely aside her married surname, she wrote in the space provided the family name of her father, becoming with one stroke of the pen the child of the mother and father who had given birth to her.

"You are asked what your religion is," said Gissa. "What shall we write?"

"Why, Jewish, of course," she replied, as if the query had surprised her.

No one saw the face of their brother Avraham when this was reported to him on the telephone. It must have borne the same expression that her father would have had, had he lived to know it. A heartfelt "Blessed be His Name" were the only words that came across the line.

The next step was the acquisition of an Israeli identity card, and despite the family's wish that Michalina herself make all the arrangements for remaining in Israel, Gissa acceded to the old lady's request that she be accompanied this time to the relevant offices.

The clerk there, turning over the pages of her Polish documents, looked suddenly up at the straight-backed aristocratic figure before him and asked her, "Are you a Roman Catholic?"

Her reply was firm and definite, "No, I am not."

Gissa, listening intently, made no comment or movement. But she treasured up the words for repetition to the family. Their value was beyond all estimation.

The clerk knew that all sorts of things had happened to the Jews of Poland during the Hitler war, and he asked no further questions.

Michalina triumphantly presented her brothers with her immigration permit and her identity card. She moved into her own room in the Senior Citizens' Home at the end of August, 1962, just about sixty years after she emerged from the convent at Bruges.

"Like a Weaned Child with its Mother"

T WO WEEKS LATER she was back in the large, green, flower-filled garden of her brother Shaye, participating in the wedding celebration of one of his children. With the memories of her mother's and her sister's betrothals still in her mind, as narrated to her during her stay in Italy the previous year, she was highly curious to see a Jewish wedding in Israel. She found the ceremony touching, especially the spreading of the *chuppa*, the velvet canopy that symbolizes the shelter of home, over the young couple. Mingling with the guests in the most natural way, an integral member of the family, no one could have guessed from her calm face and friendly manner the terrible soul-searching she had so recently undergone.

"I don't wish to feel so useless," was her next request some days later, and Yehuda, anxious for her to make closer acquaintance with people of her own age, mentioned a group of elderly women who had some knowledge of French and wanted to practice using that language. Would she volunteer to take on such a group? She agreed joyfully and it was arranged. Her brother told her, "You see, now you are making your contribution to the intellectual life of Israel."

She glowed with pride. It satisfied her that she could give of herself in this country where she had found so much warmth and peace of heart.

Reporting Michalina's return and her attendance at the family wedding, Gissa wrote to her brother-in-law Leib in New York some weeks later:

> There is no doubt about it that this is practically the first time since she was taken from her parents' home that she has lived in such a pleasant family atmosphere. She obviously appreciates it to the full. She seems to me to have had a pretty awful life and it has made her into a person used to defending herself. She is harder than most of you, not having the "butter" of your hearts.

Actually, Michalina was by nature a very generous and kind-hearted woman, especially with little children; these would bring out all the latent tenderness in her. She spoke little if at all about the lost sixty years away from the family, but she kept her pride and self-esteem throughout the years so that no one could ever treat her as a charity-orphan. Indeed, the remembrance of herself as such was something for which she could never forgive those who had imposed it upon her. With every passing week, as she became more attached to her brothers and their families, she came to perceive what kind of adolescence she had missed for no better purpose than to be turned into a charity-orphan.

"I hate poverty," she would declare with energy. So was the notion of poverty as a virtue made null and void by the very deeds of those who had tried to implant it in her.

Psychologists tell us that the ability to adapt oneself to unusual conditions and the possession of a sense of humor are the attributes that attest to the quality of one's intelligence. This strangely fated daughter of Israel had an excellent sense of humor and could certainly adapt herself; this ability had been her means of survival. The three-month probation period in the Senior Citizen's Home passed smoothly and she became a permanent resident.

From her son Karol there now came that letter mentioned previously. Addressing them as the "Highly esteemed brothers of my mother," Karol expressed his need to assure them of his joy that they and his mother had found one another. It was unfortunate, he found, that her true name had never been known to him. All her documents, attesting to her orphanhood, schooling, and nationality were made out in the name he had always understood to be hers. He had always known her to be without kith or kin, and he was already a man of fifty-six when the facts were revealed to him. It was not at all easy for him at this stage of life to discover that nothing was as he had thought. He then went on to describe his father's death-bed desire to impart something important to him. It is not hard to follow Karol's train of thought as he wrote that letter. He was probably certain now that his father had known the real origin of the girl he had married.

Michalina was immensely pleased that her son had made contact with his uncles. Contrary to her fears, her relatives and friends in Poland kept up their correspondence with her, which helped her greatly; the total separation she had so worried about did not come to pass. From time to time she would ask her relatives in Warsaw to send her various items with which she would make small, original gifts for her family in Israel. This gave her the opportunity to salve her conscience by pointing to some specific virtue of the country she had forsaken. It seemed strange that her feelings of loyalty to Poland were so much stronger than her attitude to Catholicism, the renunciation of which never seemed to trouble her any more.

"Some dried mushrooms for you," she said to one sister-in-law, "they come from the forests around Warsaw and they are so fragrant, none like them in the world." Handing her brother a book of art reproductions on his birthday, she said, "Rodakowski is such a fine Polish painter, there is none like him."

On special occasions she brought dolls dressed in the traditional Polish folk-dress for the children. She ordered a long string of pieces of amber and spent hours making them into necklaces for her brothers' wives. "Real amber from Poland," she would say.

There was nothing, in brief, that she liked better than to shower little gifts on those she grew to love so much.

Almost without being aware of it, she slipped into a completely Jewish way of life. She enjoyed the cycle of Jewish festivals and Holy Days, the significance of which was always explained to her. She found herself looking forward to Friday night *Kiddush*. With her deeply developed sense of awe, her innate feeling for the sacredness of things, she was particularly impressed with the custom of ushering in a day of rest in a manner that had all the appurtenances of a long and hallowed tradition. Her self-control was nonetheless total and it was impossible to know whether any of the Jewish ceremonies and rituals aroused any memory within her.

She seemed perfectly content. To all the members of the family, her bearing was cheerful and affectionate. Whenever her brother Avraham came to visit her, he would take her aside and explain Jewish values to her though he carefully limited the scope of these discussions since she was getting on in years. The psalmist might have had one like her in mind when he declared:

"...but I have taught myself to be contented, like a weaned child with its mother; like a weaned child am I in my mind."

Nevertheless, as *Chanuka* of 1962 approached, Michalina's family began to worry that she might secretly miss the Christmas festivities or that, witnessing *Chanuka* candles being lit and listening to the old, surely familiar melodies, she might suffer if memories of a far-off past were suddenly aroused. So Shaye and Gissa invited the family and friends to a special *Chanuka* meal — this "first anniversary" of the whole terrible chapter — and when they heard the guests arriving they quickly put out the lights. When Michalina and the company walked through the darkened living room into the dining room, they found rows of multi-colored lights strung across the ceiling, shedding tiny, twinkling spots of light on the table. This, naturally, was graced by the small candles upright in their gleaming, silver *menora*, and was laden with the traditional *Chanuka* goodies.

Michalina gasped with delight. They needn't have worried about her. She missed nothing as the beauty of *Chanuka* impressed itself upon her senses. The affair had come full circle this winter as the candles were blessed and the brothers chanted the song of Israel's faith in God through all the troubles that had come upon the nation during its long history. That evening there was so much relevance in the words:

"...by harsh oppressor captive taken, because strange gods I served there.... When Israel's power extended, the foeman's race was ended...."*

And here the story could be brought to its close. Evil had been done and had been righted. In today's world, this brings more satisfaction than the heart can express. But having followed Michalina so far, we may go the rest of the way with her.

The following year Michalina's brother Leib and his wife came from America to settle in Israel, thus enlarging the family circle. Her brothers had children and grandchildren. The daughters of her gassed sisters had managed to get out of Poland and had immigrated to Israel "illegally" during the war period. These nieces, who now lived in Tel Aviv, could talk Polish with her and chat about places in Poland and the Polish way of life. She derived great pleasure from this. Thus, although she spent the greater part of her days among people of her own age-group in the Home, she was kept young and lively by being the center of a large, attentive, three-generation family.

In this way, the years passed quickly and pleasantly for her. She enjoyed taking walks on the Carmel, and if the weather were bleak she would go once around the block just the same, telling her brothers later in her funny idiom that "today she had only gone once around her nose" (*einmal um die Nase*) for the sake of the fresh air. She

---

*The form of *Daily Prayers...* in prose and verse, Vienna, 1922... 'with the newest translation in prose and verse.'

visited the family and was visited often, and she was photographed on every possible occasion so that even her vanity was gratified. She rarely spoke of her deceased husband, however, and the family never had a mental picture of the sort of man he was. She didn't even have a photograph of him. And over the years her Polish patriotism waned as the growth of the youthful State of Israel took hold of her.

Michalina's eightieth birthday in May 1966 saw her sitting proud and upright in her brother's garden with all the family gathered around her. They had made her a surprise party, telling her nothing beforehand except that she should put on her prettiest dress. Her joy increased with every family member who came up the garden path to greet and congratulate her.

"I am too old to have a birthday party," she protested happily, and was answered in the words of the Bratzlaver: "The old bring stability to Israel and give good counsel to the people."

But after that, the hunger for her own children, so carefully restrained during the years in Israel, began to engulf her as she became aware of her age. Yehuda wrote to ask her son Karol if it was possible for him to visit his mother, and he replied that perhaps his friend, Professor P in Jerusalem, would send him an invitation to some scientific conference and then he might be able to get an exit visa. There never ceased to be an element of surprise and even mystery in this tragic episode. For this Professor P, whom Karol had known for some years and with whom he had kept up a correspondence after they once met in Europe, turned out to be none other than a cousin of Michalina and her brothers. Though neither had known it, the sympathy between the two men had been rooted in something deeper than common scientific interest.

The invitation was forthcoming, but before the formalities and arrangements for Karol's visit could be implemented, the Six-Day War broke out and the Iron-curtain countries broke off their diplomatic relations with Israel. The visit was no longer possible.

This came as a great disappointment to Michalina. It went so deep that the old lady lost much of her liveliness and began to fail from then on. Slow and gradual as the change was, it made itself clear and the ongoing process eventually made it necessary for Michalina to be placed in a hospital about seven years after she had come to Israel. Now, of course, she was no longer free to come and go as she wished, and as soon as she sensed the restriction, she regressed to her childhood. She would sit and cry, in the voice and tone of a thirteen-year-old child, "Father, Mother, take me home. I want to go home. You cannot keep me here by force. Let me go home! Why do you keep me? I want my home." Her voice would rise to a crescendo that only her father could have recognized. "Father, Father, take me home!"

Her nurses in the hospital thought it natural that she wanted to go home, but her brothers understood her better. Only now it was too late to assure her that she really was home, she had nothing more to fear.

She died quietly in July 1969, and was given Jewish burial. Surely, this daughter of Israel now rests in peace, her soul at peace with itself.

★ ★ ★

Michalina has since been joined by her brothers, Avraham and Yehuda, and, more recently, by her sister-in-law Hannah. A letter of condolence from Michalina's Italian nephew arrived but a few short weeks after Hannah's demise. In it he recalled his first meeting with Yehuda in Holland, and how it came to him that this must have been his aunt's relative. He went on to tell that Karol suffered a stroke soon after his mother's death and has been an invalid ever since, and that Michalina's favorite granddaughter recently married an Italian and went to live in Italy. It would have been comparatively easy now for them to have met again.

Excerpts reproduced from the Zionist newspaper *Die Welt* and the Hebrew journal *Hamagid* which appeared at the time of Michalina's disappearance. At her family's request, Michalina's surname has been deleted.

Nr. 23   „Die ✡ Welt"   Seite 7

Am 30. December 1899 verschwand die noch nicht viezehnjährige Tochter Michalina des Krakauer Kaufmannes Israel .... während die Eltern in der Synagoge weilten, aus dem väterlichen Hause. Noch am selben Tage erstattete der besorgte Vater bei der Krakauer Polizei-direction die Anzeige von dem Verschwinden des Kindes. Am 31. Decemcer erfuhr er, dass Michalina sich auf Zureden einer im Hause beschäftigten Frauensperson in das Kloster der Felicianerinnen begeben habe. Herr .... verfügte sich sofort in Begleitung eines Polizeicommissärs in das Kloster und verlangte seine Tochter zu sprechen. Die Oberin, Schwester Marie Rosalia, versprach, seinen Wunsch zu erfüllen. Michalina wurde in das Nebenzimmer gebracht, und der Vater hörte das Schluchzen seines Kindes hinter der geschlossenen Thüre. Gleich darauf erschien die Oberin allein und bedeutete Herrn ...., er möge nach fünf Tagen wiederkommen, das Kind müsse sich erst an die Umgebung gewöhnen.

Zwei Tage später richtete .... eine Eingabe an die Polizeibehörde, in welcher er unter Berufung auf § 145 des allgemeinen bürgerlichen Gesetzbuches um die erforderliche Assistenz ansuchte, damit er sein Kind sehen und sprechen könne. Trotz der klaren Bestimmung der erwähnten Gesetzesstelle, wonach die Eltern berechtigt sind, vermisste Kinder aufzusuchen, entwichene zurückzufordern und flüchtige mit obrigkeitlichem Beistande zurückzubringen, lehnte der Polizeidirector Korytkiewicz die angesuchte Intervention mit den Worten ab: „Was, ich werde ein Mädchen aus einem Kloster herausnehmen?" Erst nach neuerlichem Einschreiten ....s wurde ihm der Polizeicommissär Tomaschik mitgegeben. Die Oberin verweigerte auch diesmal die Vorführung Michalinas unter dem Vorwande, dass dieselbe krank sei. Als der Polizeicommissär bemerkte, die Mutter des Kindes sei schwer krank und wünsche dasselbe vor ihrem Tode noch einmal zu sehen, erwiderte die Oberin: „Sie wird sie im Himmel wiedersehen."

Auf Verlangen des Vaters begaben sich der Gerichts-arzt Dr. Filimowski und Universitäts-Professor Zulawski in das Kloster und beide Aerzte constatierten, dass Michalina vollkommen gesund sei. Erst nach neuerlichen dringenden Vorstellungen .... s wurde Polizeicommissär Tomschik am 22. Jänner angewiesen, in aller Form die Vorführung des Mädchens zu verlangen. Die Oberin antwortete: „In sieben Tagen wird sie ihr Vater sehen können." Als der Beamte die Schwester Marie

Rosalia auf die Gesetzwidrigkeit dieses Vorgehens aufmerksam machte, entgegnete die Oberin: „Wir werden uns beim Gerichte bemühen, dass die Herausgabe verzögert werde, bis das Kind das Alter von 14 Jahren erreicht haben und der Taufe kein gesetzliches Hindernis im Wege stehen wird. Inzwischen wird sie von hier weggeführt werden." Der Beamte begnügte sich damit, diese Antwort stillschweigend entgegenzunehmen und protokollarisch festzustellen.

Als .... am festgesetzten Tage des 29. Jänner sich bei der Polizeibehörde einfand, lag eine Meldung der Schwester Marie Rosalia vor, wonach Michalina zwei Tage vorher, am 27. Jänner, angeblich aus dem Kloster entflohen sei. Die Unwahrheit dieser Behauptung ist durch Zeugen festgestellt. Vielmehr war das Mädchen von zwei Felicianerinnen, deren eine den Namen Isidora führt, aus dem Krakauer Kloster entführt und in das mit diesem affiliierte Kloster Lagiewniki bei Podgorze gebracht worden. Die Anwesenheit Michalinas in Lagiewniki ist durch die dortige Gendarmerie constatiert worden, die jedoch ohne directen Auftrag, sich der Entführten zu bemächtigen, nicht einschreiten wollte. .... wendete sich an den Bezirkshauptmann von Podgorze um obrigkeitlichen Beistand, allein dieser reiste erst nach Lemberg, um sich beim Statthalter Grafen Pininski Rath zu holen, und als er von dort zurückkehrte, war Michalina aus Lagiewniki verschwunden. Seither hat der verzweifelnde Vater sein Kind in verschiedenen Klöstern, so in Binczice, Morawice, Wolajustowska, Kenty und Wielowies gesucht, allein überall haben die politischen Behörden die verlangte Assistenz verweigert und kaum hatte der Vater den behördlichen Organen den neuen Aufenthalt seiner Tochter zur Kenntnis gebracht, wurde das Mädchen sofort in ein anderes Kloster geschickt. Nur in Kenty leistete der Bürgermeister Herrn .... die im Gesetze begründete Assistenz. Er wurde dafür wegen Hausfriedensbruches zu 10tägigem Arreste verurtheilt, welches Urtheil das Appellgericht von Wadowice aufhob.

Nachdem so die politischen Behörden sich ihrer gesetzlichen Verpflichtungen beharrlich entschlugen, nahm .... am 1. Februar 1900 beim Justizminister Freiherrn v. Spens-Booden Audienz und trug demselben die inständige Bitte vor, ihm auf gerichtlichem Wege zu seinem Kinde zu verhelfen. Der Justizminister entliess den tiefgebeugtsn Mann mit den trostvollen Worten: „Fahren Sie ruhig nachhause, das Kind soll Ihnen zurückgegeben werden." Der Justizminister beauftragte unverweilt die Staatsanwaltschaft Krakau, beim dortigen Landesgerichte die Strafanzeige wegen Entführung zu erstatten und den Antrag auf Ausfertigung eines gerichtlichen Auslieferungsbefehles einzubringen. Die Rathskammer des Krakauer Landesgerichtes in Strafsachen lehnte unter dem Vorsitze des Präsidenten Moralewski diesen Antrag ab und verweigerte später dem Rechtsfreunde .... s die verlangte Einsichtnahme in die Acten mit folgendem Decrete:

„Zahl VIII 395/900

$\overline{155}$

Herrn Prof. Dr. Josef Rosenblatt, Landesadvocat, Krakau.

Ohne die Frage zu entscheiden, ob Israel ....
in dieser Sache als Privatbetheiligter anzusehen sei,
wird die Einsichtnahme in die Acten in der Angelegen-
heit der Michalina .... verweigert, weil wichtige
Gründe dem im Wege stehen. — Ihre Vollmacht wird
zur Kenntnis genommen.

Krakau, den 29. März 1900.

K. k. Landesgericht in Strafsachen.

Wawrausch m. p."

Am 14. Februar trug Israel .... seine Sache dem
Ministerpräsidenten Dr. v. K o e r b e r vor, welcher auf seine
Bitte um Schutz erwiderte: „S i e v e r d i e n e n e s, e s
g e b ü r t I h n e n."

Dagegen antwortete am gleichen Tage der Minister
für Galizien Dr. P i e n t a k 'auf die Bitte ....s, zu
seinen Gunsten zu intervenieren, mit den Worten: „A n
d e n M a u e r n d e s K l o s t e r s h a t d i e w e l t l i c h e
M a c h t e i n E n d e."

Nachdem alle Bemühungen, von den galizischen
Behörden Hilfe zu erlangen, fruchtlos geblieben waren,
suchte .... um eine Audienz bei Sr. Majestät dem
K a i s e r an, welche ihm am 26. April huldvoll gewährt
wurde. Der Monarch geruhte, die ihm überreichte Bittschrift
aufmerksam durchzulesen und sodann an den unglücklichen
Vater, der schluchzend vor ihm auf die Knie sank, die ver-
heissungsvollen Worte zu richten: „I c h w e r d e n e u e
W e i s u n g e n a n d i e B e h ö r d e n g e b e n, d a m i t
d i e s e i h r e P f l i c h t u n d S c h u l d i g k e i t t h u n !"
— Diese Weisungen sind auch thatsächlich schon zwei
Stunden nach der Audienz ergangen, aber trotz der Ver-
heissung des Kaisers hat noch am 8. Mai d. J. der Bezirks-
richter Edmund H a r t m a n n, als .... ihm zur
Anzeige brachte, dass seine Tochter im Kloster zu Wielowies
bei Tarnobrzeg gesehen worden sei, jeden Beistand mit den
Worten abgelehnt: „Gehen Sie zum Staatsanwalt,
e r s o l l e i n e n A n t r a g s t e l l e n, u n d u n s e r e
S a c h e w i r d e s s e i n, d i e s e n A n t r a g e b e n s o z u
v e r w e r f e n, w i e e s i n K r a k a u g e s c h e h e n i s t."

Am 17. Mai hat .... diese Thatsache dem
Justizminister und am 19. Mai dem Ministerpräsidenten zur
Kenntnis gebracht und sowohl von Baron S p e n s als von
Dr. v. K o e r b e r die Zusicherung erhalten, dass im Wege
der galizischen Statthalterei alles aufgeboten werden wird,
um den Aufenthalt seiner Tochter n o c h v o r d e m
27. M a i, an welchem M i c h a l i n a das religionsmündige
Alter erreicht, auszuforschen u n d i h m s e i n K i n d
z u r ü c k z u s t e l l e n.

Der 27. Mai ist herangekommen, aber Michalina
.... befindet sich noch immer im Kloster. Mit dem
voraussichtlichen Religionswechsel ist, nach einer Reihe
von Präcedenzfällen, die Gefahr verbunden, dass die
Vormundschaftsbehörde dem Israel .... die väterliche
Gewalt aberkennt, obwohl eine solche Entscheidung im
Gesetze nirgends begründet ist. Dann wäre das Kind seinen
Eltern für immer verloren.

Nr. 8   HAMAGID L'ISRAEL   שנה תשיעית

בחיר החתימות
שדר קורד 50 קרוצר וחצי רחבה 80 כ־
סאריא ב־חי חתוברים בבית
המקריט ליב סיב ואב לכב־לוט
הזידו הזרלי.
יעקב שמואל פוכם.

Erscheint jed. Donnerstag

הארכרטת אל בית המערבת
Redaction „HAMAGID"
KRAKAU (Österr.)

אורגן לכל דורשי־ציון
עתון לאוב לכל עניני ישראל.
חשפה הטשלות שגהב.

מחיר החתימות
באוסמריה־אונגרוט
לשנה 12 קראיב, לחצי שנה 6
קראיב לרבע שנה 3.00
באשכנו:
לשנה ... 12 סארק.
לחצי שנה רבי החתימה.
בצאר ארצ״ת ...
לשנה ... 20 פראנק.
לחצי שנה לפי החשבון.
טיסמנרורק של חיר רב יקנבל.

Krakau. 23 Februar, 1900   גליון ח.   קראקא. כ״ג אדר, התרס.

קראקא. ר׳ ישראל _____ אשר בתו, ילדה בת יד שנים, נעצרת בבית מקלט הגזירות זה, ינע עד כה לריק להוציא את בתו ואף לראותה ולדבר אתה נגע ממנו. הילדה נחמה על מעשיה וכוכה ומיללת כל הימים, ע״כ אין את נפש הגזירות לתתה להראות את אביה. כאשר לא חדל האב האמלל להפציר בהגזירות לחביא לפניו את בתו, שלחוה מביתן אל עיר אחרת ומקומה לא נודע. בשבוע שעבר הלך _____ עם אחד מקרוביו ועם ציר בית מעצוה העיר חין הדיר ש ט י ר ן להתחנן לפני המעיסטר יועל המשפטים ולשני ראש הממשלה הדיר מן ק י ר ב ר בדבר בתו. שני המנים־פרים שמעו בשום לבב את דבריהם ויבטיחו לחקור ולדרוש בדב־ וביעי את תקותם, כי פקידי המשטר י ע ש ו ב ו ד א י את חובתם. האב האמלל התמתג כמעט בדמעות בהיכלי המעים־פרים, ותקותו לדוציא את בתו מבית מעניה לא הזקה, כי ידוע שיד חברת נזירות בנליציה חזקה מיד פקידי המשט־.

———

קראקא. ב״ב הדר ב־ק העיר בישיבת „הילוב ,סולני ,האחרינה יבוה ע״ד הנעיד _____ אשר הגזירות בקראקא אחזות בה ביד הזקה וממאנת לבסוה ליד אביה, ישאל את המעיסטר פינטק, אם הממשלה לא תהיו ישע להאב האמלל. המעיסטר ענהו, כי כבר נעשו צעדים שונים בקרית הענין הזה וכי הישעות הבקוםית תעשה כל אשר בכחה להשיב את הנערה לבית הוריה; אך לע״ע כל הצעדים לא ישאו פי. ואם גם לפי השמועה נמצאה כבר הנערה בבית הגזירות בלאגיוונ־ק! הסמך ל פ ־ ה נ ־ ר ־ י בכ־ה לא עלתה עוד לאביה לראותה, והוא מוטיח להתאמיץ בכל מאמצי־כחי להציל את בתו מיד עושקיה.

———

קראקא. ישראל _____ אבי הנערה הגתתיה בבית נורים, התיצב ב־חד עם הרב הגאון ש מ ל ק ם בלטוב לשני הנצב נראב סינינסקי יתאו־ לפניו את צ־תו, כי זה חדשים הוא נע נע עד בארין לבקש את בתו ועוד לא מצאה, ולפי דב־י הנזירה מ־א ־וזליה כי הנזירות להשמים את הרב־ ולהסתי־ את הנערה עד אחר חדש מאי, שאו ימלאו לה יד שנה, ולא תהיה במוסה עוד לאביה. הנצב השיבו, כי ל א י עזו־ ז למעשי חמס וישע, אבל סקנו הנערה לא נודע לאקידי הממשלה. לפי השמע כלתה נפש הנערה בימים האחרונים לראות

את אבותיה ותוגא לקראקא דבית הגסיסה סוסיצקו. — ביום 28
לחדש העבר הגישו האגנ־ססטים בבית ועד המדינה בלבוב כתב־מחאה
להגציב לקרוא תג־ על מעשב השוטרים, שחששו בכתי הגדרים את
הנעיה. _____ וישאלוהו, אם כבר נטסיח השוטרים כדי רשעתם. —
בסודניד־ז־ כ־חה עוד נעיה עביה בת י"ב שנה, גולדפינג־
שטה, לבית הגזירות.

_____

קראקא. בחדש הזה תמלאנה לבת ר' ישראל _____ י"ד
שנה ולא תהיה עוד תלויה בדעת אביה בדבי המ"ח הדת. כאשר נלאה
האב האמלל להדיש את בתו ביד השוטרים ובתי המשפט גם אחרי
שהתיצב לפני המניסטרים ולפני נציב נליציה לבקש צדקה ומשפט,
נסה גם את הצעד האחרון: להתיצב לפני הקיסר יר־ה ולבקש ממנו
עודה. ביום ה׳ לשבוע העבר התיצב לפני הקיסר ויתחנן אליו, לאמר:
.דוד מלכות, בת י נגזלה מביתי והיא נשלחה ממקום למקום. מרחמי
הוד מלכותך, צדקתו וטוב לבו אבקש עזרה! לו יואיל דוד מלכותך
להביע בחסדו את חפצו, כי ישיבו לי את בתי, אקוה מזה עוד לישועה,
ועד יום מתי אתהלל על שלום דוד מלכותך. הקיסר ענהו: .הרבר
**נודע לי מעם ועוד אחקור על הדבי. הלא עשו בתי הפקודות את
הובתם ?׳** ויען _____: .המניסטר שעל המשפטים נתן פקודות נמרצות,
אבל לא נודע מי שולח יד להבי עצתו". הקיס־ שאל, אם יודע הוא
את מקום בתו עתה, ויעי״ _____, כי לדעתו עודנה בל"ס במדינה.
_____ הוסיף להתחנן בבכי ויאמר, כי אשתו חולה ונהביא לבתי
מענה בלתי טוב, אז ינזום זה מות לאשתו. בהשתהבות נפש נפל
לרגלי הקיסר. הקיס־ צוה לקום ויאמר: .אנכי אשלח פקודות
חדשות להשוטסים, למ ע ן יעשו את חיב זהט".

_____

קראקא. בעתון הפולני "Słowo Polskie", נדפס מכתב מד־
ישראל _____ בו מודיע, לאמר : .בהודע לי', כי בתי נמצאת בבית
הנזירות בוייעלאהישט הסמוכה לטרנובזג, שלחתי שמה איש להדיש שם,
אם אמת הדבר. כאשר הודיעני האיש, כי ראה את בתי שתי פעמים
נטעתי שמה עם אהד מטכיר. בהויתנו עוד בדרך תשאלנו שוטר־ העי־
טרנובזג ואחריונו בתואנה, כי אגנו יכולים להוכיח מי הגנו אחר־ כ־ד
שעות יצאתי לחפשי ואלך אל ש־ הכהה לקביל לפני גם לחלות
בני להרישות אותי להכנס לבית הנזירות. ש־ המחה שלחני אל שופט
המחה, אשר עננו, כי בלי פקודה מקטעיר המעיטלה לא יכל לעשות
דבר, ואשוב ריקם מטרנובזג כאשר באתי שמה והאיש אשר נלוה
אלי במסעי עודנו אסור בטרנובזג." — קול נשמע, כי המניסטר לעניני
הדתיה שלח פקודה לכל הגמוני אוסטריה, לבל יביאו את הנעיה
_____ בברית הדת הנצרית רק עד מלאות לה כ׳ד שנה. אם אמת
הדבר, אז יש תקיה, כי יצלה לאביה להשיב אליו את לב בתו, אבל
לדעתו פקודה כזאת לא תוכל לצאת רק בצרון הקיסר, כי ע״פ החוק
יכולה נעיה יהודית להמ־ר את דתה במלאת לה יד שנה, וע״כ עוד
הרבי מוטל בספק.

❦ הַשָּׁבוּעַ ❦

צִיד נְפָשׁוֹת בְּגַלִיצְיָה.

הַנַּעֲרָה _____ אָבְדָה לְאָבִיהָ לְשָׁלֵם וּלְמָרוֹת הַבְטָחַת הַקֵּיסָ׳
בִּכְבוֹדוֹ וּבְעַצְמוֹ וּלְמַרוֹת פְּקוּדָתוֹ הַנִּגְזָרָה לְכָל בָּתֵּי הָאֲסֵקוֹרוֹת אֵין עוֹד
תִּקְוָה לְהָאָב הָאֻמְלָל לְהָשִׁיב אֵלָיו אֶת בִּתּוֹ הַנִּגְזָלָה מִבֵּיתוֹ. אֲבָל הָאָב
הָאֻמְלָל הַזֶּה אֵינֶנּוּ הָאֶחָד וְהַמְּיֻחָד. עוֹד יֶשְׁנָם בְּגַלִיצְיָה כְּמַעַט בְּכָל עִיר
וָעִיר אָבוֹת נָאֱנָחִים הַנֶּאֱנָקִים כָּמוֹהוּ וְאֵין מוֹשִׁיעַ.

❦ הַשָּׁבוּעַ ❦

צִיד נְפָשׁוֹת.

אָכֵן נוֹדַע הַדָּבָר : בֵּית הַגְּוִירוּת הַמִּילִיצְאַנְזִית בְּקְרַאקָא הוּא מְצוּדָה
פְּרוּשָׂה עַל כָּל מְדִינַת הַסָּלוֹנִים לְצוֹדֵד שָׁמָּה נַעֲרוֹת יִשְׂרָאֵל מֵהָעֲרִים
הַקְּטַנּוֹת וּמֵהַכְּפָרִים. מְצוֹדְדִים וְסוֹכְנִים שְׁכוּרִים מִתְהַלְּכִים בְּאַרְצוֹת פּוֹלִנְיָה
לָקַחַת שְׁבִי אֶת בְּנוֹת הַיְּהוּדִים וְהַגְּוִירוֹת בּוֹטְחוֹת בְּכֹהֵן הָעִיר וּבְהִתְרַשְּׁלוּת
בָּתֵּי הָאֲסֵקוֹרוֹת נֶגְדָּן לְהוֹסִיף חַיִל וְלְהַרְבּוֹת מִסְפַּר שְׁבִיּוֹתֵיהֶן מִיּוֹם לְיוֹם.
בִּשְׁמוּעוֹת הָרִאשׁוֹנוֹת מִסְקָרִים בְּאֵלֶּה הָיוּ יְכוֹלִים לְהַאֲמִין. כִּי רַק נְעָרוֹת
אֲחֵרוֹת, קְלוֹת דַעַת, נִסָּתוּ לְעֵצַת מְאַהֲבֵיהֶן וְהַגּוֹיְרוֹת רַק שׁוֹמְרוֹת אֶת
הַנְּעָרוֹת הַבָּאוֹת אֲלֵיהֶן בְּרָצוֹן : אַךְ הַמִּקְרִים הַחֲדָשִׁים יְלַמְּדוּנוּ, כִּי אָמְנָם
הַגּוֹיְרוֹת שׁוֹלְחוֹת מַלְאֲכֵיהֶן לָשׁוּט בָּאָרֶץ וְלָקַחַת שְׁבִי נְעָרוֹת גַּם בְּחָזְקָה.
וּבְזֶה נוֹסְפָה לְצָרוֹת אַחֵינוּ בְּגַלִיצְיָה מְצִיקָה חֲדָשָׁה, שֶׁאֵין כָּל עֵצָה לַעֲמֹד
נֶגְדָּהּ, וְאֵין לָנוּ מַה לַעֲשׂוֹת רַק לִשְׁמֹר אֶת בְּנוֹתֵינוּ בִּשְׁמִירָה מְעֻלָּה
מֵהַלֹּךְ בְּסַח יִקְשׁוּ לָהֶן מְשַׂנְאֵינוּ. הַמִּקְרִים הָאֵלֶּה נֹדְעוּ בַּשָּׁבוּעַ הַזֶּה :
בְּיוֹם הַכִּפּוּרִים הָעָבַר בָּאוּ שְׁלֹשָׁה אֲכָרִים לְבֵית הָאַלְמָנָה חַנָּה זַוִוירֶר
בַּוְולָא ־ שְׁטְשׁוּם שִׁינְסְקָא סָמוּךְ לְטַרְנוֹב. הָאִשָּׁה הָיְתָה בְּבֵיהַ״כְּנ
בְּעִיר שְׁטְשׁוּם שִׁין וּבֵיתָהּ נִשְׁאֲרָה לְבַדָּהּ בַּבַּיִת. הָאֲכָרִים לָקְחוּ אֶת
הַנַּעֲרָה שְׁבִי וַיּוֹלִיכוּהָ לְקְרַאקָא וַיִּמְסְרוּהָ לְבֵית הַגְּוִירוֹת. הָאִשָּׁה בָּאָה
בְּחֶרְדָּה גְדוֹלָה קְרַאקָאָה וְכָל עֲמָלָהּ לְהִכָּנֵס אֶל בִּתָּהּ הָיָה לָרִיק, וַתֵּשֶׁב
בְּאֵין נֶפֶשׁ אֶל מְקוֹמָהּ, וַמֵּיוֹב יָגוֹן אֲחָזַתָּהּ מַחֲלָה עַזָּה וַתִּפּוֹל לְמִשְׁכָּב
וְלֹא יָכְלָה עוֹד לַעֲשׂוֹת רַבְ׳ לְהַצִּיל אֶת בִּתָּהּ.— בִּדוּבְשְׁטִיצָה פָּתוּ
שְׁתֵּי נָשִׁים תֻּרְפִּית אֶת בַּת הַיְּהוּדִי אֵלִיָּהוּ מֶנְדֶל יִסְפִּינְגְלְסוּדֵעַ לְבְרֹחַ
קְרַאקָאָה. פְּעָמִים אֲחֵרוֹת בָּא אָבִיהָ לְקְרַאקָא וְהַגְּוִירוֹת לֹא נְתָנוּהוּ לָבוֹא
לִרְאוֹת אֶת בִּתּוֹ וְכַאֲשֶׁר הֵפְצִיר בָּהֵן הָאֻמְלָל בִּכְבוֹדִית וַתְּתֻנוּת שְׁלָחוּהוּ אֶל
הַהֶגְמוֹן הַנֶּסֶךְ פּוּזִינָא, וְהוּא שְׁלָחֵהוּ אֶל הַמִּינִיסְטְרַאט וּמִשָּׁם נִשְׁלַח
אֶל הַשּׁוֹטְרִים — וְכָל עֲמָלוֹ לְטָוְא.— נַעֲרָה אַחֶרֶת, נ.ע.ל.ב שְׁמָהּ
מִיַּזְוִיעֶרְטְשׁוֹב, הִצְלִיחָה לָנוּס מִבֵּית שְׁבִיָהּ אַחֲרֵי אֲשֶׁר עָנוּהָ
שָׁם יוֹתֵר מִשְּׁלֹשָׁה יְרָחִים. הִיא סִפְּרָה, כִּי יָשְׁבוּ אִתָּהּ אֲסִירוֹת שְׁתֵּי נְעָרוֹת
מֵאוֹלְיַה הַרוּסִית, שֵׁם הָאַחַת אלסמאן וְשֵׁם הַשֵּׁנִית לְדְרְמַאן, וְהֵנָּה
בּוֹכוֹת וּמְיַלְּלוֹת כָּל הַיָּמִים.

* * *

קראקא. הנגף פטמיסלא מאדנובסקי ודר׳ ציל׳ ערבו
מחאה אל נשיא המניסטריום ושר המשפטים בדבר הגזרה הנעלמה
_____ אך לא לטובת אביה האמלל, חלילה, כי א ל י־ע ת ו: על
חטא שחטא בבקרו יחד עם פקידי הפוליציה את בית מקלט הגניזית
והקרו ודי־שו שם אחרי בתו באופן בלתי נאות. ולמען הוכיח את עזות
היהודים ספרו הנבחרים האלה גם ע״ד המאורע, שקרה לפני ב׳ שבועות
בעירנו להגזרה הזאת מוויליטשקא (ראה נליון 9). ובהוספם על המקרה
הזה בחל וקרק כיד דמיונם האנטסמיטי הטובה עליהם הגיעו
לפני המניסטריים את השאלות האלה: א) הידעת הממשלה מכל
המקים האלה והכונה היא לעני־ט את הנאשטים – היהודי _____
והיהודים שלקחו דברים עם הממרית מוויליטשקא – בשעתם
כ) ומה בדעת הממשלה לעשות ליטים ליבואו לעזרי לעזיר בעד
משוכת היהודים נגד בתי הגניזית להקתיליס?
הנה כן על הממשלה לעני־ט עוד את היהודי _____ על
הטי־ לחפש את בתו – איט־ לא מצאה עוד לביתה כל יפי־שו
ואת היהדים הנאשמים בעין פגיעה בגמטרית מוויליטשקא הנאספים
זה כבר במאט־ ומשפט קטה צפו להם גם בלעדי מהאת
הנבחרים הנגל! והנה רא על "ישר־לב" ט־נובסקי יצי־ל
אנחנו מצטעים, כי הן כבר הרגלנו לטמוע מהאות כאלה וכאלה
ספי צורינו! אך על זה תאבל נפטנו בזרכנו, כי צורי־נו הנובים
נבחרו לבית המחזקקים רק בעירה – יטמעו והשתוממו! – "נטיא"
קהלתנו והשפעתם, כמו טנבזר "אוהבנו" פינטק לבית הנאמנים
יטליצי רק בהטד־לות נטיא קהלת לבוב הר־ ב׳ ק ומעני־ היהדינ.

_____

קראקא. בסוף מאמרנו הראטר בנליון הקדם נתנו מקום לקוראיס –
בלתי מבינים – בעירנו לנלות פנים שלא כהלכה, כמו הפצנו לפנע
בכבוד הר־ר ישראל _____ כי לא חנך כמשפט את ב ת ו, אשר
ננזלה בידי זדים, ובאמת לא כן הוא. בשם "מעשה" _____ רגלים
בעת העתנים לציין ב כ ל את ציד נפשות בנות ישראל, אשר חזיונו
נפרץ בימים האחרונים, ועל ה ר ו ב אמנם החנוך המשחת אשם בזה,
אך ה׳ ישראל _____ יוצא מן הכלל הזה, כי הוא חנך את בתו על
ברכי היהדות הטהורה ומע בה משארית של ילדותה נטעי נעמנים, ואם
למרות זאת קרה לו האסן, לא בו האטם תלוי. ב ת ו י ו ד ע ת ה י ט ב
ע ב רית ואהבה את עמה בכל לבה וק ביד חזקה נזלוה מזרועות
הוריה האמללים, אשר כב־ הוצאו סכום עצום להצלתה – וכל עמלם
לשוא, ליק ולבהלה! הקיס־ יריה בכבודו ובעצמו הבטיח את האב
האמלל לחקיר ולדריש, וגם אמנם היתה החקירה והדרישה בעזית כל
הפקידים הרמים והנשאים והכל – לשוא! כאי הנראה נמצאה עוד
הנעיה _____ באחד מבתי הגניזות בנליציה, וכ־יז קשה למצאה
ולהדותה...